War on Poverty

War on Poverty

HUMWOPO

By Senator Hubert H. Humphrey

McGraw-Hill Book Company

TORONTO
LONDON
NEW YORK

War on Poverty

Contents

Contents

War on Poverty

1 / *The Paradox of Poverty*

This is the revealing and paradoxical story of today's America—a country of unprecedented wealth and prosperity that harbors in its midst 35 million people without sufficient food, shelter, and clothing. It is the story of one out of five Americans who live in poverty, shame, misery, and degradation.

It is also the story of people who cannot be separated from statistics, and whose plight is never fully realized unless you see the hopelessness on their faces and the plea in their eyes.

Four years ago, during the presidential primary in West Virginia, I visited a town whose sole source of income—a coal mine—had been closed. The houses and stores in the town were dilapidated, the people wandered about aimlessly.

I was having breakfast with some of the townspeople, discussing their problems and trying to inject a note of optimism into the conversation, when a tall, spare, shabbily-dressed man whose face had turned red from the cold walked in the door and came up to me. I shook his hand and said, "I'm Hubert Humphrey. I'd appreciate your vote in the election."

The man looked me in the eye—I shall never forget that look—and said, "Yes, I know, Senator. I need a job, any kind of a job. I've got three kids and they're hungry. Is there something you can do about that?"

That spring in West Virginia I met thousands of men looking desperately for work, each man's face reflecting bewilderment and need. And every time—every single time—it hurt.

Among the people who write to me from Minnesota is an elderly woman from Saint Paul. She is without family or friends and has nowhere to go, nothing to do. In the summer when the weather permits she walks about the city but during the winter, forced to stay indoors, she spends her time writing letters to her senator. With a cash income of $63 a month—more than the median benefits received by widows under Social Security—she has barely enough money to pay her rent. Her existence depends upon surplus food distributed by the city and old clothing she receives from charitable organizations.

Testifying before a Senate committee, a sheriff from West Virginia described the effect of loss of jobs and opportunity on the people in his county:

I have had so many men, honest men I have known all of my life, come into me in my office and make the statement they wouldn't let their children starve if they had to steal. Some actually are stealing food; some are making moonshine. And some men are even going into the mines and cutting wire down, hot wire with juice in it, and stealing copper and going off and selling it to provide for their families. . . . I have passed along the garbage dumps where stores throw their garbage out and I have seen little kids eating discarded apples and stuff from the garbage dumps. And it is heartbreaking to see these things.

The Sheriff went on to say that much crime occurred in his county.

It is pitiful. And it is caused by people being out of work. I have people coming into my office day after day with small children. They can't send them to school. They have nothing to go on. They don't have any clothes or shoes to wear. They don't have any food in the house. . . . And just as I said before, people in my county are proud. They are honest people and good people and they don't want a handout from the government. They don't want a handout from anyone. They want an honest living; they want something to do, to work and to make an honest living. And how we can do that, God only knows. It is up to the people in the government to try and help us do something in my county.

Here is a statement from a county superintendent of schools in West Virginia who testified before the same Senate committee:

We know of many, many cases where the only meal that those children have during the entire day is that balanced

meal at noon at the school cafeteria. A great deal of that
meal is surplus commodities that we are now getting from
the federal government and without that, these children
would go hungry. That is their only meal, many of them.

He also brought out that in some instances a
child would take milk or maybe part of his school
lunch home to a younger brother or sister who
was hungry.

This is part of the testimony of a woman who
has been engaged in welfare work for more than
twenty-five years:

They want work. They want work that produces; they
don't want work that is merely set up as a plan instead
of assistance. They want work that produces a commodity
that is useful, that is needed, that boosts their morale, and
is an incentive to make better citizens.

A man came into the office not too long ago and he said,
"Lady, I am not disabled, and I don't want assistance.
But," he said, "look at these hands. Have they been used
to an easy life? Aren't they toil-worn?" They were,
gentlemen. There were calluses all over his hands. He
said, "I am forty-five years of age; I have two children
in high school. The rest of my children are in the grades
and they can't go to school because they are unable to
have shoes."

Another day a woman came in. She said, "Lady, my
husband was ashamed to come into the office. He has never
been without work. But," she said, "when I left home
this morning there were five children who were hungry
and I can't go home." It was then a few minutes before
five o'clock. She said, "I can't go home without some kind
of food."

Gentlemen, I ask you, can we afford to let any children in America go hungry?

Here is the statement of still another county school superintendent:

One little first-grader came to school one morning pale and vomiting. The teacher suspected that she had not had anything to eat that morning and asked her if she ate breakfast. She said, "Yes." The teacher said, "Did you eat some hot cereal?" She said, "No, Mother didn't have anything but chow-chow." This is a local concoction of late, green tomatoes, cabbage, peppers, etc. made into a kind of pickle relish.

These examples and thousands of others describe not only a material and physical poverty but one equally destructive—a poverty of the spirit.

The man without a job, without any opportunity to care for himself and his family develops a sense of bitterness and rejection. He is poor. His friends and neighbors are poor. He is surrounded by a culture of poverty.

The stark figures and statistics offer a challenge to the American people and their way of life. Why among the industrialized nations of the world does America the richest nation in the world have one of the highest rates of unemployment and the least security for its elderly? How can we be content with some of the dirtiest cities, the most crowded streets, and the most shameful slums? How in a world half colored can we continue to deny educational and economic opportunity to our own colored citizens? How can we continue to keep 35 million of our fellows beyond the boundaries of even a minimum existence?

Americans have never run from a challenge. Instead of wringing our hands over past failures we have always taken the initiative, rolled up our sleeves, and worked for what we wanted. Despite the fact that prior to the Japanese attack on Pearl Harbor we were totally unprepared for war, we became the arsenal of the Allied advance. Our genius for planning and management enabled us to use the great productive capacity of the free-enterprise system and meet attacks from both sides of the globe. After the war was won, by setting our sights high and calling upon all the elements of a free society to work together we rebuilt the economy of Western Europe, we invested money and technological assistance to strengthen the democratic way of life in Latin America, Japan, and the emerging countries of Asia and Africa. Now these countries are prospering, and many have a higher employment rate than our own, and are competing against us vigorously for world markets. Surely we can do as much for our own people.

We must harness the same brain power and capital resources to fight the war on poverty. As rich as we are, we cannot afford the waste of slums, the drag on the economy that stems from unemployment and rising welfare costs, the crime, disease, and vice that are the by-products of poverty.

Government alone cannot solve the problem. Political leaders can stimulate goals, make speeches, write books, and introduce legislation, but in the final analysis it is the union of government, private industry, and free labor which gets the job done. Every significant social change in the history of America has occurred because the conscience of the majority of the American people was aroused. In order to achieve a truly productive economy and eliminate poverty we must have bold and imaginative ideas and the courage to put those ideas into action.

There is a poem by Emma Lazarus inscribed on a tablet inside the pedestal of the Statue of Liberty that epitomizes the hope of America:

> "Give me your tired, your poor,
> Your huddled masses yearning to breathe free,
> The wretched refuse if your teeming shore.
> Send these, the homeless, tempest-tost, to me,
> I lift my lamp beside the golden door!"

America has always stood in men's minds as the hope for a bright new society. Today, with the economic resources and brain power at our command, we can give expression to that hope by creating a nation of abundance. We stand at the threshold. Let us open the golden door!

2 / *The Dimensions of Poverty*

In preparing the 1964 Economic Report of the President, the Council of Economic Advisers regarded as poor a family unit of four whose annual money income from all sources was less than $3,000 (before taxes and expressed in 1962 prices). To get its cut-off figure of $3,000, the Council relied on a study made by the Social Security Administration which set up a minimum, economy-plan budget for a non-farm family of four at $3,165. This minimal standard is the lowest I have personally seen from any reputable economist.

Among many commentators who quarrel with the figure of $3,000 is Walter Lippmann. He says:

This is not enough money to maintain a decent standard of living for the family. If the family spends 70 cents a day per person, it will spend a little over $1,000 a year on food. That leaves $2,000. It is estimated that $800 will be needed for housing—rent or mortgage payments, utilities and heat. This leaves $1,200. That is less than $25 a week for the whole family for everything else—clothing, transportation, recreation, medical care, insurance.

Though $3,000 a year would be affluence in a village in India, it is harsh poverty in the United States.

Let us examine figures supplied by the Bureau of Labor. In terms of 1961 dollars, the Bureau has estimated that the cost of a "modest but adequate" level of living (excluding taxes) for a working-class family of four persons in New York City was about $5,200 in 1959. Using these figures it becomes apparent that we are not discussing one-fifth of a nation that is poor, but the one-third of the depression years.

It is not difficult to see that definitions of what constitutes poverty are subject to controversy and confusion. Any standard of poverty must by definition be an arbitrary one. What is important is for us to realize the extent of our problem and to know that there are thousands of families in addition to those technically classified as living in poverty, but who also exist on the ragged edge of subsistence. We must capture the real meaning of poverty and experience what it is like to be an internal alien in the America that is taken for granted by the rest of us. Only then will be plight of the poor be seen in detail and the impact of their terrible condition arouse the public as no statistical exhortation could possibly do.

For our purpose the poor are those people who

are not maintaining a decent standard of living with respect to the society they inhabit—those families or individuals whose basic needs exceed their means to satisfy them. The arbitrary figure of $3,000 will be used both as a means of demonstrating need for imminent action, and for its consistent use as a base for studies on poverty made by various government and research facilities.

During 1963 there were 47 million families in the United States. Fully 9.3 million, one-fifth of the total, had incomes below $3,000. Translating these figures into numbers of people, this means that in rich America, we have over 35 million persons living in "official" poverty. What is even more tragic is that this figure includes some 20 million children—one-sixth of our youth—whose parents cannot give them enough to eat, cannot clothe them properly, and cannot afford proper medical and dental treatment. To compound the enormity of these statistics, 5.4 million of these families containing more than 17 million persons and more than 8 million children had total incomes of less than $2,000.

Take a walk through the rooming-house district of your city and notice the lonely people gazing aimlessly out their windows. These are the so-called "unrelated persons"—men and women living on meager pensions, social security, family charity. The bitter facts of poverty among unrelated persons is equally startling.

In 1962, 5 million people, forty-five per cent of people living alone or in non-family units such as boarding houses, had incomes of less than $1,500 and one-third, twenty-nine per cent, received a total income under $1,000.

Who are the poor? Where do they live? Why are they poor?

The problems of poverty are not new—they have been the concern of economists, sociologists, and legislators for many years. Yet until President Johnson's State of the Union address in January, 1964, and his message on poverty to the Congress on March 16, 1964, brought to bear the enormous prestige of the Presidency, the plight of the poor was all but invisible.

In declaring "unconditional war" on poverty, the President reminded the complacent among us that the unprecedented prosperity which most of America enjoys is "a hollow achievement."

The President said:

Today, for the first time in our history, we have the power to strike away the barriers to full participation in our society. Having the power we have the duty. . . . On similar occasions in the past we have often been called upon to wage war against foreign enemies which threatened our freedom. Today we are asked to declare war on a domestic enemy which threatens the strength of our nation, and the welfare of our people.

If we now move forward against this enemy—if we can bring to the challenges of peace the same determination and strength which have brought us victory in war—then this day and this Congress will have won a secure and honorable place in the history of the nation and the enduring gratitude of generations of Americans yet to come.

As late as the eighteenth century people were arguing as to whether or not "those miserable persons were worth their keep." The reigning philosophy, as expressed by Mandeville, was that "The poor have nothing to stir them up to be serviceable but their wants, which it is prudent to relieve, but folly to cure. . . . To make society happy it is necessary that great numbers be wretched as well as poor." Even by the end of the nineteenth century, most people thought that nothing public policy could do would lessen the condition of the poor. There were even a few who advocated that it was bad policy to relieve the burdens of poverty.

In our own country, it took the great depression of 1929 to formulate policy that made public welfare, unemployment compensation, and security for the aged generally acceptable. These programs, while not curing the causes of poverty, alleviated much outright misery.

Why is it that the power of the Presidency was needed to spotlight the condition of one-fifth of our nation?

In 1929, half of the families and individuals in the United States had incomes below $3,000, in terms of 1962 dollars. Today, the middle class is twice as large, much more affluent, and able to escape from the ghettos of poverty that blight our cities. It is not difficult for the majority to ignore our 35 million poor. To most of us the poor inhabit a sector of society that we hardly recognize. They may come to do the laundry or fix the garden, but we barely see them as we speed by on the freeways or ride the commuter specials to and from the cities. For many of us the only poor man we notice is the fellow posted for non-payment of bills at the country club.

Mesmerized by a highly productive economy, we tend to assume that everyone must be participating. Our standard of living keeps going up, over-all per capita figures keep climbing, and many neighborhoods are virtually free from poverty as we have defined it.

Isolated from the mainstream of society, the poor are without most of the things the rest of us take for granted—light, heat, warm clothing, educational and economic opportunity. The poor have no way to advertise their plight. They have no union to press their interests, no lobby to pressure for reform. Even among those working, only about one-quarter belong to a union.

Michael Harrington, author of *The Other America: Poverty in the United States,* makes the interesting point that America has the best-dressed poor the world has ever known. Mass-produced clothing is the cheapest of the necessities and, paradoxically, cloaks the misery of the poor, making them even more anonymous.

Our poor do not just inhabit the back alleys and attempt to eke out a bare existence on our farms.

They are also our sick. Four poor people are disabled by chronic ill health for every one of the relatively prosperous. For the poor, illness is a catastrophe. They have little to spend on medical care; nothing if one accepts the Social Security Administration's minimum "economy plan" budget. This is an even more serious problem for the aged poor who are the most prone to illness. During the 1950's the Consumer Price Index went up twelve per cent but the costs of being sick went up thirty-six per cent.

Largely as a result of ill health among the impoverished, the United States ranks substantially below a number of other countries, particularly those we helped to rebuild in Western Europe, in average life expectancy and nutrition, and higher in infant and maternal mortality rates.

If the poor, who are four times as sickly, cannot afford to be physically sick, the costs of mental illness are completely beyond their means. Yet, the incidence of mental disease increases as you go down the economic ladder. A recent study made in New England showed that the rate of "treatable psychiatric illness" for the well-to-do is 573 per 100,000 persons. Among the bottom fifth it triples.

It is more expensive to be poor. Those on the lowest economic scale almost never pay cash, even for the most basic necessities. Everything is on credit. They pay the high cost of installment buying.

Marvin Jones, Chief Judge of the Court of

Claims, tells this story about being poor. Judge Jones is the son of a tenant farmer from what the Texans call "hard" country. He recalls going to the bank with his father to borrow money. They negotiated a three-month loan at an interest rate of ten per cent a month. When they left the bank he asked his father, "Why did you borrow the money for only three months? We won't have the crops to pay it back by that time."

His father said, "The banking system of this country is set up for the businessman, not the poor man, and don't you ever forget it."

The poor are bad credit risks and as a result suffer from the high cost of borrowing money. In addition to installment buying they are often forced to go to loan sharks who command an exorbitant return, thus perpetuating the cycle of poverty. Whenever I am in a poor community or slum, I am astonished by the differences in price. I have often seen a pair of socks selling for a dollar and a half or more in a place like the south side of Chicago that would cost less than half that price at the Mart. Furniture that looks as though a stiff breeze would blow it apart is offered at outrageous prices.

The poor are different in respect to attitude and outlook. A few years ago a governmental study made by a team of psychiatrists investigating the poor in a city of 170 thousand people described them as follows: ". . . rigid, suspicious, and have a fatalistic outlook on life. They do not plan ahead. . . . They are prone to depression, have feelings of futility, lack of belongingness, friendliness, and a lack of trust in others.''

The poor are also isolated. Michael Harrington says that the percentage of people in the lowest economic class who are without affiliations of any kind is eight times as great as in any other income level. This characteristic is again most prevalent among the indigent old. They huddle indoors, out of sight, in run-down houses on back streets. Their children cannot care for them, much less attend to the wants of their own families.

The effect of this total alienation of the poor from the rest of society is to breed the culture of poverty we mentioned in the preceding chapter. In the struggle to survive, there are few moral values, no ends except individual maintenance.

After looking at the facts, I submit that no moral man can ignore the plight of such people. If morality and conscience are not enough, the simple cost of poverty in dollars and cents should be a compelling enough reason to initiate action.

We hear a great deal about the cost of our welfare programs. Let us take a look at the hidden costs.

We pay for the poor not once or twice, but three times. First, society loses the production of wasted human potential. Second, the poor have little or no purchasing power. And third, we divert necessary funds to alleviate misery in the form of various welfare payments.

Our direct expenditures in relief payments and unemployment compensation are over 6 billion dollars a year for food, clothing, and shelter. And this amount takes into consideration only those people who apply for and get some form of governmental assistance. This enormous burden on the rest of the country could be considerably larger because only one-fourth of those classified as poor receive unemployment compensation or welfare help.

Welfare and public-assistance programs such as Unemployment Compensation, Workman's Compensation, various veterans' benefits, Old Age Assistance, and Aid to Families with Dependent Children involve transfer payments—taxes paid by the rest of the country which are transferred through various agencies to the poor. To the funds contributed by the federal state and local governments we must add the enormous sums of money spent to alleviate poverty by charitable and private foundations. I have never seen authoritative figures but I would estimate that they must total an additional 10 billion dollars.

We suffer other indirect costs as well. David L. Baselon, Chief Judge of the United States Court of Appeals for the District of Columbia, recently said:

We are beginning to realize that the rising crime rate is not caused merely by weak law enforcement. Poverty in all its manifestations—a lack of basic necessities, family breakdowns, mental disorders, unsupervised youths,

school drop-outs, alcoholism, drug addiction, and so on—
is the chief factor producing anti-social behavior. From
my own experience, I know that most defendants con-
victed of crimes of violence in the District of Columbia
are indigent. A successful war on poverty would come
close to solving the crime problem.

The hidden costs of poverty in terms of crime
are considerable. A recent study of a slum area
in New England showed that forty-eight per cent
of school drop-outs, almost all poor children, were
either arrested or referred to juvenile court
shortly after leaving school. The costs of law
enforcement, detention, and rehabilitation are
much greater in slum areas.

Poverty and ill health constitute a vicious cycle.
Poverty denies the poor adequate medical attention and sickness generates even more poverty.
The U.S. National Health Survey has found that
persons in low-income families are more apt to be
absent from work, are more often badly disabled,
and, in the case of children, lose more time from
school because of ill health. On an average, the
poor lose close to twice as much time from work.
The great sums of money we spend each year
in welfare pales before the hidden loss in productivity and national income which we lose
through continued poverty and unemployment.

If we were to add only $500 a year to the earned
income of our eleven million families now living in
the bottom layer of poverty, we would put an additional 5.5 billion dollars a year into circulation.

This additional 5.5 billion dollars would actually give an extra thrust of over 20 billion dollars to our national economy. This is because of what the economists call the "the multiplier factor." According to this theory, every additional dollar put into circulation changes hands several times a year.

Consider for a moment only the financial aspects of our poverty problem. By failing to eliminate poverty we have limited our domestic market to only about four-fifths of its potential—not including the multiplier factor. Simple arithmetic demonstrates that the majority of Americans would be even better off, increase their profits, dividends, and salaries, if there were no pockets of poverty, unemployment, and underemployment. The largest potential market in the world is not in Asia, Latin America, Africa, or the Common Market, it is here at home. We can tap it whenever we wish by making productive, income-earning citizens out of our poor.

If the moral implications of poverty and the plight of the economically vulnerable is clear, and if we understand the staggering cost of poverty, the next question is, can we afford to do something about it?

We now enjoy an economy of enormous resources. The facts almost defy imagination. During the first quarter of 1964, we had 68 million persons employed and produced a Gross National Product—the value of all our goods and services—

of 608.5 billion dollars—an increase of 8.5 billion dollars from the first quarter of 1963. Personal income during March of 1964 projected an annual rate of 480.5 billion dollars.

In view of these statistics, some economists have proposed a direct subsidy to the poor. The Council of Economic Advisers states that every family's income could be brought above the $3,000 cut-off point by a direct subsidy of 11 billion dollars a year to the lowest income groups.

Eleven billion dollars would be a gigantic relief check, but it is not beyond the capacity of an American economy operating at over 600 billion dollars a year. Certainly this nation could pay such a price, if need be, to provide a reasonable standard of living for all its citizens. A relief program of this magnitude would amount to about one-fifth of the yearly defense budget, and less than two per cent of our gross national product and would be less than ten per cent of our tax revenues.

Economist Milton Friedman, a strong conservative and adviser to Senator Barry Goldwater, argues for such a subsidy. He calls it a "negative income tax." As Mr. Friedman envisions it, a direct subsidy would avoid the creation of a new federal bureaucracy, and would also be a strong argument for removing, or at least reducing, other subsidies while leaving the poor free to use their money in ways that seem most effective to them— without government interference.

Other economists argue for a similar subsidy in the form of guaranteed annual income. This should not be confused with the guaranteed annual wage presently operating in some industries. They say that just as we have accepted the idea that all Americans are entitled as a matter of right to receive an education, all Americans should be entitled to a guaranteed cash income.

I have serious doubts that these methods are desirable. There are better alternatives. We shall always have among us those who cannot work, and we must accept the responsibility of helping them. Our task lies, however, in creating meaningful jobs for those who are not helpless. Even if it were to cost society more to provide jobs instead of doles or handouts, it would be a better solution. The fact remains, however, that the real costs of providing productive work would be far less than either a dole or subsidy. The same productive capacity which enables us to afford an 11-billion-dollar welfare bill, coupled with the untapped market represented by the poor will produce enough jobs and goods and services to bring abundance within the reach of us all.

In order to achieve maximum production we can no longer refuse to see the poverty before our eyes. The figures and case histories, the repetitive facts about poverty, can no longer bore us. We can no longer afford the short-sightedness of dogma and the stupidity of inertia.

3 / *Investing in America's Future*

In April, 1964, President Johnson spoke to a U.S. Chamber of Commerce meeting in Washington. To these businessmen he said:

In this political democracy, what you have and what you own and what you hope to acquire is not secure when there are men that are idle in their homes and there are young people adrift in the streets, and when there are thousands that are out of school and millions that are out of work, and the aged are lying embittered in their beds.

Outside of the poor themselves, the American businessman has more at stake in the war against poverty than anyone else.

Business cannot prosper in a society at war with itself; it has already been hurt by the refusal of some elements in this country to recognize the rights of the Negro to equality of opportunity. The productive capacity of the impoverished and the huge potential market that their untapped consumer purchasing power represents will be wasted unless steps are taken right now.

Over the past several years we have had a very high unemployment rate on the Iron Range in northeastern Minnesota. In spite of everything we could do in terms of federal and state action, it looked as though unemployment would continue indefinitely without the help of some major private investment and the consequent employment of several thousand more people in the iron mining business.

At that time, a constitutional amendment to encourage investments by the steel companies in our taconite deposits was being hotly debated. The steel companies would not commit themselves until the state of Minnesota passed the amendment providing for an open-ended, indefinite period for the tax incentive. Positions were hard and fast on all sides. Dogmatic thinking was blocking thousands of job opportunities for the region. I decided to contact the chairmen of the boards of two major companies, who, in addition to Minnesota were considering investment in major taconite plants in Michigan and Wisconsin.

After a series of separate meetings with these men we secured public assurances that if a self-terminating constitutional amendment providing tax incentives over a twenty-five-year period (rather than a permanent program) were adopted in Minnesota, they would commit several hundred million dollars to the construction of taconite plants without delay. Negotiations and bargaining had overcome dogma. The results were guarantees on both sides and the prospect of several thousand year-round jobs for a deeply distressed area. This represents the kind of joint venture and cooperation increasingly needed between government and industry.

In addition to the billions of dollars we have spent since World War II rehabilitating what we destroyed in Europe, we have spent even more billions rehabilitating depressed areas all over the world in the name of the cold war.

The Marshall Plan was expensive; but we sought stable economies and stable governments in Western Europe, and we got them. Europe not only did not come under Communist domination but now represents a massive force on the very frontiers of the Communist world. We have strong and vigorous free allies—and they pay their own way. Our investment, in short, was a sound one.

In Latin America, where economic and political improvements are a vital necessity, we alone since the war have invested some 4 billion dollars. Our projected commitment of public and private resources to the Alliance for Progress is for over 20 billion dollars. During 1963 alone, the Inter-American Development Bank, to which we are the major contributor, authorized fifty-six loans in South America totaling almost 260 million dollars. With a much more primitive "infrastructure" (the necessary underlying facilities such as trans-

portation, power, etc. on which basic productive
enterprise depends), and with a far lower level of
literacy and health than in Europe, Latin America
nevertheless also represents a sound and necessary investment area for the American taxpayer
and private investor. We simply cannot afford to
abandon the rest of the hemisphere to philosophies
hostile to the United States.

If anything about poverty is clear, it is the
massive size of its problems. There is no program
limited to government alone that is politically
feasible at this time—not even a joint program
involving federal, state, and local governments—
that can do more than make a dent in the problem.
The Area Redevelopment Administration, for example, has made only slight improvements in the
over-all employment problem of the distressed
areas—in spite of heroic efforts.

Small-scale attempts to provide jobs simply
nibble at the problem. What is required are large-
scale investments which can create dramatic employment opportunities and "bootstrap" local and
regional economies. This necessitates both business confidence and government encouragement
on a large scale, either through specialized tax
incentives, government purchasing programs, investment guarantees, or the use of direct or indirect government funds as leverage.

It is sometimes asked: why invest at all? Why
not have the unemployed from a depressed area
simply move out?

We should encourage and assist those who wish
to leave a depressed area and seek opportunity
elsewhere. Government agencies are permitted to
make relocation loans and ascertain job opportunities in more prosperous areas in an effort to
relocate the unemployed, but are we really re-
signed to a policy of evacuating large sections of
this country? Are we prepared, for example, to
abandon half a state at a time?

I reject any solution that would, in effect, force
the people of these areas to cut their ties, leave
their friends, abandon the equity they may have
in their homes, and turn their backs on their
heritage.

According to the Area Redevelopment Administration, in 1963 there were 141 urban areas,
877 rural areas, and 54 Indian reservations in
need of assistance—over a thousand locations in
the United States as targets for redevelopment.
We must devise methods of utilizing the often-
excellent natural and human resources in these
areas.

Public works can provide temporary employment and strengthen the community base upon
which private investment must build. But build
the private investor must, if these distressed areas
are to resume normal economic life.

Without the opportunity to apply the skills of
men, training programs in depressed areas are
futile. A man may be the most skillful and highly
trained person living in West Virginia. If there

is no job opening for him, he will remain a highly trained but unemployed West Virginian.

The trick is to get investors, who have ample opportunity for investment in booming areas of America and other highly industrialized nations, to invest in an area presently suffering from fundamental economic problems.

The World Bank is by far the most sophisticated of all the international financial institutions and programs we have supported. It makes its headquarters in our own back yard, at 1818 H Street in Washington. It has had a spectacularly successful history in combating poverty throughout the world in the kind of depressed areas that make Appalachia and Harlem seem almost affluent.

Let us consider for a moment the way in which the World Bank operates. Chartered by most of the civilized countries of the world after the Bretton Woods Conference of 1944, the Bank had an initial authorized capital of 10 billion dollars.

The Bank's charter states that its purpose is to make loans in member countries where such loans will improve the standard of living. This is done on an area-to-area–project-by-project basis.

Politics are kept to an absolute minimum, with loans made only after a feasibility study demonstrates that the ultimate return to the economy of the area as a whole will insure repayment—the same manner in which a local bank or credit union reviews loans.

Since no single government has voting control, no one country controls policy or can exercise political domination. The Bank is run by professionals—bankers, economists, sociologists, and technicians. Last year these professionals showed a profit of some 83 million dollars, plus another 90 million dollars plowed back into reserve and operating funds.

There are two overriding rules: The Bank wants its money used well, and it wants to be paid back. Not one loan has ever been defaulted.

The Bank has outstanding over 7 billion dollars in loans. Less than a third of this balance represents its own money. Two-thirds of the funds have come from the sale of its bonds to private financial sources or from the sale of participations in its loans to the private sector.

The Bank does not initiate projects and keeps hands off local policy. Although the Bank may advise and consult as to desirable projects, and even engage in some promotional activity, all projects and applications are originated locally. The Bank reviews them to make certain that they will make a substantial contribution to local living standards and that they are economically feasible.

The underlying theory of the Bank in stimulating economic development has been to concentrate on making loans to basic projects—infrastructure projects—which will in turn generate what might be called ''creative earning power'' to provide the framework which supports the rest of the area's development. It also makes loans to productive business facilities that will serve as stabilizing financial entities within an area.

In short, the World Bank represents a sophisticated, business-like approach to the problems of world poverty—and it works.

Many Americans hold to the myth that our native ingenuity and energy were alone responsible for the fantastic speed with which we developed our nation. True, we were ingenious and energetic. But equally important was the fact that by the end of the nineteenth century *European* investors had put 3.7 billion dollars into the American economy. Until 1900, America was an underdeveloped debtor nation. To a very great degree, it was the injection of this outside capital that laid the base for the twentieth-century American economy.

Outside capital, via the World Bank, is transforming many parts of the world today. Take Ciudad del Carmen on the Mexican Gulf, for example. Men used to loaf in the streets because there was nothing else to do. No road connected it with the rest of Mexico.

The people of Carmen used to fish for shrimp in a "fleet" which consisted of two decrepit boats. A few of the town's more enterprising citizens thought that there might be a possibility of exporting shrimp, but they needed ice. Carmen's primitive power plants could barely turn out the ten tons of ice its two small ships required each week.

At 200 pesos a ton—which was more money than many of Carmen's 12,000 inhabitants saw in a year—the operation was uneconomical. Carmen itself was an economic zero.

That was twenty years ago.

Today, when you land at the new airstrip, you find a miniature boom town. New retail stores have opened up along broad new avenues. Taxis rattle on the streets. There are two modern hotels. A new town hall has been built, and the two movie houses have had to enlarge their seating capacity to take care of overflow audiences. At night the streets are lit.

On the piers the change is just as apparent. The shrimp fleet is a fleet indeed now, with more than 200 boats in operation.

In a generation Carmen has stepped out of the past into the present. The secret was in the financing of generators providing 2700 kilowatts of electricity. For Carmen this meant adequate and reliable supplies of power—power to make ice for its fishing boats, power for its local industries, light for its streets, energy for its telephones, radios, and electric fans.

Carmen obtained its generators through a World Bank loan. It was a relatively small loan, but it is being repaid. It has brought prosperity and jobs to a pocket of poverty in Mexico.

Why not to Harlem, West Virginia, the Ozarks, the Upper Peninsula of Michigan? It *can* happen here.

We might well profit from the World Bank's experience and give consideration to establishing some sort of domestic investment bank to function in our distressed areas in much the same way the World Bank operates abroad. Let us assume that development techniques similar to those used in Ciudad del Carmen were applied here. Consider as an example a typical, American location—any one of a hundred desolate towns.

Until recently this town was a one-industry community depending on the coal mines for survival. The sale of coal brought money into the town—money for the operators to spend and money for the miners. The town provided services to every man on the payroll—which would include not only the miners themselves, but the bookkeepers in the office, the stenographers, and the talley clerks. Gas stations, movie houses, the hotel, the stationery store, the bank and, in turn, all *their* employees depended on the town's basic productive enterprise—coal mining. But today the mines are closed.

How long can the people in this town survive selling services to each other? Cutting each other's hair, repairing the grocer's car? Not very long, because they are living on a sort of localized barter system. No money is coming into the community from the outside world. They have an area "balance-of-payment" problem, for they must purchase goods and commodities from the outside. Since their own basic productive facilities have been shut down, no funds flow in. Sooner or later, this area barter system will collapse.

But suppose a new industry were introduced, a new productive enterprise to replace the coal mines—an electronics plant, perhaps, or a textile mill—anything that could compete effectively and that would put the men back to work and at the same time ship products to the outside. I suggest that this town would boom again, as did Ciudad del Carmen and that the men could return to work and maintain themselves and their families, and, in turn, the families of the men and women who provide the services in their town.

It has been suggested that if this enterprise were financed by some kind of domestic investment bank the local bank might complain at the competition and interference which, after all, would be to some degree federally supported.

I doubt it. This is not the kind of relatively short-term loan in which conventional bankers are primarily interested. I suggest also that the First National Bank of our mythical town would be anxious to have the town restored to economic life. It would mean payroll deposits, individual checking and savings accounts, and a growing opportunity on the part of the local bank to make personal loans, give mortgages, and, in general, re-invest in the community.

I do not mean to suggest that every town is readily susceptible to a new industry. But most pockets of poverty can support some type of new, creative, productive enterprise. The World Bank has found this to be the case throughout the depressed areas of the world.

In order to make sure that they are getting the job done and to give the right kind of help where help is needed, the World Bank maintains a technical assistance program. This includes a staff college, providing training in problems of economic development, and a corps of economic and technical advisers.

Nor has job training of the local citizenry been ignored. In recent years the Bank has moved into education, building technical schools (and public schools) in areas where they believed there has been a paucity of skilled workers.

To alleviate any fears about domination from Washington, the federal government, for example, might subscribe to less than fifty per cent of the capitalization of such an investment bank and various states, private financial institutions and individuals be offered the balance. The bonds of such a bank backed up by federal and state subscriptions might well be marketed through private channels. Participation in such a bank's loans might also be made available to the financial community. They would probably be acceptable.

This kind of program makes sense to me. It is an effective joint venture between government, the financial community, and business and labor. Politics are out. It makes a profit. It gets results.

The Economic Opportunity Act of 1964 already
provides for the establishment of local groups to
initiate plans for self-improvement. These community plans—which might see a need for hydro-
electric development; feeder roads; educational
institutions; new, basic industrial facilities, depending on the area in question—should be a basis
for project loan applications to such an institution.

If we are to call on the experience of the World
Bank, loan criteria and considerations such as
these come to mind:

1. A pocket of poverty would be involved.
2. The investment or credit would tend to raise
   living standards in the community in question.
3. Local governments as well as private entities
   would be eligible as borrowers.
4. Ability to repay either directly or through
   the local taxing power might be one but not
   the only criterion.
5. I would give such a bank the authority to
   guarantee loans made by the private sector.
6. I do not think I would distinguish between
   big-business and small-business applicants.
   Many of these projects are reasonably massive and would require big business.
7. The loan guarantees of local governmental
   entities might also be encouraged.
8. Rates should be low and terms flexible.

9. Such an institution might consider the extension of credit as part of the project for use in training prospective employees of the facility.

We have federal programs, such as the Small Business Administration and the Area Redevelopment Administration. They have been established to perform similar functions on a small scale. Various states and local entities have other programs to stimulate new business. I am in favor of these and would like to see them strengthened.

The Small Business Administration has as its primary concern small business and not the infrastructure or more massive, productive programs. In addition, due to congressional carping, it has avoided risks in America's future to the extent that its loan policies have become, until recently, increasingly restrictive.

The Area Redevelopment Administration has tried to do too much with too little. It is over-governmentalized, requiring layer after layer of government decision—local, state, and federal. Present congressional authorization for it is strictly limited to 100 million dollars at any one time in urban areas and another 100 million dollars in rural sections. It has been suggested that the program be doubled, but I doubt whether even a 400-million-dollar program will go far to eliminate poverty in the over 1,000 localities designated as eligible for redevelopment. This would mean an average of less than $400,000 an area.

If we could be successful in inducing private participation and can promote a local partnership, I believe we could bring a much more massive program to bear with a greatly lessened burden on the federal treasury.

A bank functioning as I have outlined might accomplish much in a co-operative fight against poverty without the problems that have confronted the existing, purely federal, agencies. It might very well become one of the more effective weapons available to us in the war against poverty.

I have mentioned guarantees. We have been successful with the use of government guarantees to private investment in the past. The Federal Housing Administration used them to stimulate the housing boom that has been going on since the war.

We should use the guarantee device more often to stimulate the investment of private funds into those areas of the economy that need help. This is a fundamental exercise of "leverage" in the kind of joint venture I have been discussing.

What we need, above all, is a willingness on the part of business, labor, and government to sit down not only to settle a railroad strike, but to do some constructive planning.

People who are against this sort of planning are really against federal domination—and in part, they are right, because the planning needs to be done on a joint-venture basis. Planners from business, labor, and farm groups need to come together with men and women in government to make policies which will encourage investments and stimulate economic activity that will be of benefit to the nation. Planning for a region must take advantage of the knowledge and experience of those who live there, work there, and plan to stay there.

But to plunge headlong into a major undertaking without making some estimate of the total cost, some estimate of a goal and the number of years to accomplish that goal, without setting up a framework for decision-making and a line of authority to get capital committed, and decisions translated into action is simply foolhardy. No successful war was ever fought without planning.

We learned a great deal from our experiences with the Marshall Plan and from foreign aid in general. One lesson was that enough capital must be budgeted over a long enough period of time to permit the efficient planning and use of that capital.

We also learned that there must, indeed, be planning at the top, but also from within.

We learned that there must be regional planning.

We learned that capital must be supplemented by technical assistance.

We learned that we needed both government loans and private government-insured loans.

We learned that we needed a friendly climate for private investment, because government could not do the whole job.

We learned to demand country and regional plans—not just project plans—for it did not make much sense to duplicate certain existing facilities in adjoining countries.

We learned the need for centralized planning and direction and decentralized operation.

We learned that it is not always desirable or necessary to set up new mechanisms or departments of government, but that a task-force approach which called on the resources of existing agencies could be more efficient.

We should take advantage of the experience of the World Bank.

What we must now do is to follow President Johnson's favorite admonition: "Come, let us reason together."

That is the key. Together, forgetting the old hostilities between businessman and bureaucrat, management and labor, we can make the kind of effort our times require.

4 / *Urban Poverty*

By all odds, in terms of dollar income, the worst poverty is found in rural America. There are counties in the South, close to the rich TVA country, where you will see mile-after-mile of shacks without running water or plumbing where the people live in rags. Scarcely anyone can read or write. Families are living in the same kind of poverty that the rural poor of the nineteenth century knew.

But the slums of the great cities—to which so many hundreds of thousands of refugees from the poverty of the rural South have fled—are more wretched, more degrading, more soul-destroying. More than half of the poor—some 20 million people—live in metropolitan centers.

City dwelling, even for those not forced to live in the slums, is rapidly becoming a poor way to live for many people. It is scarcely a decent way of life when you are afraid to walk the streets alone at night. Our cities are overcrowded; the slums are chaotic and ugly; transportation systems are inadequate. Many of those living in the suburbs spend two to three hours a day simply journeying to and from work—about a sixth of their waking hours. The nuclei of the cities are literally dying—areas to be avoided, if possible, for the dirt and disease and crime.

And yet, year by year, we are becoming a more urban nation.

When I was elected to the Senate in 1948, the population of the United States was 150 million. Since that time we have added more than the total population of Great Britain. By 1975, there will be 225 million people; by 1980, 250 million.

Our population is moving, as well as increasing. During the 1950's alone, the population of states like Florida and Nevada increased by over 50 per cent. Arizona, Alaska, California, and Delaware grew at the rate of 20 to 40 per cent. At the same time, Arkansas, West Virginia, and Mississippi lost population at the rate of 20 per cent or more. By 1980, more than three-quarters of our people, a sum greater than our present population, will be living on 10 per cent of our land area in giant cities primarily around the sea coasts and the Great Lakes area. The heartland of America is being drained.

The shift of people off the farms and out of the small towns has already denuded tens of thousands of square miles of rural America. Farm-to-city movement, particularly by young people, is being accelerated by economic forces that make it difficult or impossible to maintain a family on a farm at a reasonable income level. The population of rural America grows older. The rural poor are already flooding the cities and adding to the ranks of the urban unemployed. Policies designed to further encourage this move only compound the already mounting difficulties of the big-city slums.

For all practical purposes, these rural emigrants now crowding into the slums are as helpless (and as exploited) as the nineteenth-century immigrants from eastern and southern Europe or the Puerto Ricans coming into New York City today. A sharecropper from South Carolina or Mississippi who migrates to the ghettos of Chicago or Detroit finds it every bit as shocking an experience as it was for the European immigrant the day he landed in New York. At least the Europeans came in hope and optimism; they saw in America the chance for new opportunities. The emigrant from Mississippi who has been pushed off his land by machines travels to the city with despair and foreboding. To him the city is a foreign land—a strange and alien environment.

Most of these new emigrants, both Negro and white, are truly technological illiterates. Without industrial skills and the experience to adapt to the noise and stress of the city, they become just additional bodies jammed into more tenements. They have no family or community ties; not even the predictable pattern of their former lives.

The poor-white differs from his Negro coun-

terpart in only one respect; the color of his skin
saves him from the additional burden of discrimination. In all other considerations he is just as
lost. Poverty is a great equalizer. It creates for the
rural emigrant a community of misery where unemployment and crime flourish.

Nineteenth-century America was a fairly broad-
based nation. There was regional, cultural, economic, sociological, and political diversity. In this
century we are rapidly becoming a monolithic
urban culture that is tending to stratify into two
classes: inner-city poor, suburban better-off. The
colors of the great city are black and white: inner
city is colored; suburban is white.

Even the suburbs, the backwash of the wave that
choked the cities, are spreading at such a pace and
with such a rate that they constitute a kind of
brush fire, seemingly uncontrollable and surely,
at present, uncontrolled. The reasons which motivated people to move out of the city to the suburbs
—privacy, room, air, light—are rapidly disappear-
ing as the suburbs continue to grow. Suburbs have
their own harassments and their own emptiness.
Lacking both the cultural resources of the central
city and its economic resources, they are described
by critics as a strange village in the daytime,
occupied by women and children, by those same
people and their tired husbands, at night. The
malaise which has descended like a fog over suburban life may not concern us today when other
more pressing problems attract our attention; but

if it persists, the often unsatisfactory way of life produced by suburban living will become a major national problem.

If the present pattern of white suburbs and colored "core cities" continues, we will be faced with the prospect of political and economic struggles between black cities and white towns and suburbs.

An America of racial discrimination and *de facto* segregation is a house divided against itself. Urban America can well be torn apart by the explosive power of resentment and hatred. Metropolitan areas that are essentially black centers ringed by the wealthier whites cannot safely be permitted to crystallize and solidify.

One difficulty in doing anything constructive about such a situation is the incredible political fragmentation of these huge urban areas. These hopeless tangles of city governments, suburban councils, county and state authorities are all desperately trying to stay afloat with stop-gap measures, inadequate tax bases, uncertain jurisdictions, and with less than friendly and understanding state and federal legislators. There are 64 separate governing bodies in greater Boston. Greater Chicago has over 1,000. The New York metropolitan area has some 1,500. Over all, 180 American cities have some 16,000 such local political entities.

Local jealousies, jurisdictional disputes, the sheer communications problem among the many

separate governments of a great metropolis spell
out a formula for cynicism, despair, and an in-
evitable tendency to pass the buck. It is a conven-
ient avenue to avoid the responsibility of coping
with the core area's slums, its poor, its crime, and
fundamentally, its burdensome costs.

Some political scientists have even suggested
that we may be nearing the point at which we must
contemplate revision of our Constitution to take
into consideration the reality of metropolitan
areas whose population exceeds the combined populations of several entire states.

During my tenure as mayor of Minneapolis, I
soon learned that routine services to a slum were
many times more expensive than providing the
same service to well-to-do areas.

Los Angeles has found that blighted areas cost
the city 87 per cent more per capita in police services, 67 per cent more in Fire Department services, and 125 per cent more in health services than
more prosperous communities, while yielding only
38 per cent as high a rate of tax revenues.

With the application of intelligence and perhaps some new ideas, we may be able to turn the
very blight of the cities and their fearful difficulties into a blessing in disguise.

There are so many dwellings for poor people
that are substandard—at least 5 million living
units in metropolitan slums with an additional
10 million requiring immediate substantial repair and modernization—so many crowded and

inadequate schools, so few libraries and gymna-
siums, playgrounds and swimming pools, so many
overcrowded hospitals and limited out-patient
care, that decades could be spent in putting people
to work just to rehabilitate their own neighborhoods.

While we already have a program for urban
renewal, it is inadequate. Federal grants, loans,
and cost-sharing programs to provide for the engineering of master plans of urban renewal and
the destruction of slum areas largely finance the
massive freeway-construction programs which
bulldoze down through the hearts of the cities to
provide rapid transport for trucks, transients and
suburbanites, but often succeed only in aggravat-
ing the problems of those who live in the centers
of the cities.

The thousands of families driven from their
homes by the slum-clearer or road-builder are
left to themselves. In many cases, we are tearing
down old slums only to replace them with new
slums. We are shifting problems—not solving
them. Transferring the poor from one house to
another—even if it is to a solid, better-constructed
public housing building—only scratches the sur-
face.

Some fifteen years ago New Haven, Connecticut,
began its effort to stamp out its slum blight. The
mayor of New Haven, Richard Lee, has now been
through the urban-renewal mill and has fought
most of the difficulties, some unforeseen, includ-

ing a great deal of opposition within his own community.

Mayor Lee says that physical rebuilding has not been the city's most difficult problem. New Haven found that the long years of slum dwelling had created sociological problems that could not be solved simply by moving the poverty-stricken out of their physical misery. Many had been on the welfare rolls since the early 1930's. Second and third generations were growing up unprepared to take their places in normal society.

New Haven developed a partnership between the local, public and private sectors called Community Progress, Inc., formed for the purpose of applying brain power to the city's problems. Community Progress found sociological dislocations so drastic that it became necessary to establish a homemaking program to teach the fundamentals of family living to those moving into new dwellings so that they would not carry with them the habits acquired over years of slum dwelling. It became necessary to broaden the functions of the schools to include teaching parents as well as children to read, write, add and subtract. Neighborhood employment centers were established and a massive campaign launched against school drop-outs.

Community Progress found that knocking down old buildings and putting up new ones was not enough. The poverty-stricken were so steeped in misfortune that they lacked the inner resources to recover by themselves.

For many people in New Haven poverty is no longer invisible. Community Progress, Inc. took a hard look, used imagination and thinking, and, instead of wringing its hands, went about attacking the problem.

Mayor Lee says, "You can't win the war against poverty with stirring slogans. You have got to have earthy people willing to take on the dirty work."

For some years, many of the country's finest minds have been discussing how the metropolitan centers of the future should be planned. Some advocate a policy of complete decentralization. Others argue for the creation within the cities of what amounts to self-sufficient villages such as are found in Rotterdam and, to a lesser degree, in London.

Certainly slum clearance alone is no answer. Slum clearance and sensible rebuilding must include plans for industrial parks located near housing, as well as schools and parks.

Industry and business have demonstrated a tendency to move away from the metropolitan cores, but the people of the slums lack this same mobility and are unable to find new jobs to replace the jobs lost by industry's relocating. Through the creation of large industrial parks in the center we might reverse or, at least, slow this trend.

People often talk about the "crowded" slums. To some degree this is true, but there *is* space, both vertical and horizontal. You can see this space as you walk through these areas. In spite of the crowded conditions, there are numerous empty buildings and lots. Empty lots and structures are a characteristic of most slum neighborhoods. Besides being run-down, the houses have fallen into such a state of disuse that they emphasize the look and feel of poverty. The broken windows in the burnt, condemned, and abandoned houses, and the lots filled with weeds and rusting pieces of metal stand as a challenge to ingenuity.

Even on a temporary basis, without master planning and huge investments, much can be done to use these resources of open space and idle manpower. Playgrounds can be created and maintained, and a few trained professionals may be able to motivate and guide many of the idle and the elderly who would gladly do some constructive work and supervision in their neighborhoods. The problems of working mothers, or employable mothers, in the slums be could eased by the establishment of day-care centers for the children, so that these women may go about their work knowing that their children are in safe, competent hands. This day-care center program should become an integral part of urban growth and planning.

We should provide for, on as much of a self-help basis as possible, recreational facilities particularly geared to the tastes of the aged—where they can meet and gossip, read, or enjoy a game of cards, and, if necessary, a place where they can stay.

In addition, we should develop a citizenship program which will educate those at the lowest economic level to the positive aspects of law and law observance. Most of the poverty-stricken fear the law as their enemy, not their friend.

Neighborhood legal clinics which would assist with income tax returns, small claims, housing code enforcement, marital disentanglements and reconciliations, insurance claims, social security benefits, financial management, loan agreements, and workmen's compensation, would be one device for a better understanding of the law.

But piecemeal, temporary measures should not prevent us from moving ahead on a massive scale necessary to solve the urban problem—the fact is that most of our cities need rebuilding. At the federal level, the challenge of the urban metropolitan areas is so immediate and so huge that it only makes sense to co-ordinate the present federal efforts into a Department of Urban Affairs headed by an officer of Cabinet rank. Such a department could stimulate some of the broader planning that is so clearly required. It could co-ordinate the plethora of local governments and create commissions to look at the plight of the great cities—each one of them as an entity with separate and distinct problems.

Above all, the crisis of our cities should challenge us. On one hand are the great conglomerations of the poor and the unemployed searching for constructive work; on the other hand are the problems of transportation, housing, education, medical care, and recreation that will inevitably demand extraordinary investments of capital and manpower if they are to be solved.

Here, in the very cities that hold most of the unemployed, can be a key to the solution of unemployment.

In searching for ways to put Americans to work constructively, we cannot be content simply to contemplate expanding production of television sets and steam irons or other consumer goods. What must be constantly sought are enterprises on a sufficiently large scale and with sufficient by-products to create sufficient numbers of new jobs. Everyone knows that the defense and space programs are enormous generators of jobs. For every soldier in the Army there are several civilian workers who are making hardware for the Army. For every pilot in the Air Force there are probably hundreds of workers involved in some facet of the aircraft business related to the Air Force.

National defense and the space program are also huge consumers of capital, brains, and manpower. They not only provide jobs, but also stimulate research and development. But they are not going to go on forever at the present scale.

William James was always seeking what he called a "moral equivalent of war"—some vital goal that would challenge men and women to sacrifice and work together for a higher purpose than their own selfish ambitions. In a sense, what is required is not only the challenge that will make men work and sacrifice for the good of the nation, but also an economic equivalent of war and the space race.

A cutback in arms procurement may very well be coming in the next few years, a cutback which could have a very serious impact on many segments of our economy, unless we have planned to shift our resources of capital and manpower to a constructive, civilian-oriented undertaking. In other words, we can accept a cutback in arms procurement as a blow to the economy, or we can plan to use that cutback to expand and intensify the civilian-based economy to make an attack on great areas of national concern.

Why not, beginning now, before any major arms cutbacks, think of planning the first major reconstruction of great cities since the rebuilding of Western Europe and Japan?

It is said that it would take a major catastrophe to get the diverse and quarreling jurisdictions which make up the greater metropolitan area of, for instance, Los Angeles, to work and plan together. Well, then let it be noted that a major cutback in defense procurement would be the nearest thing to a great economic catastrophe that Los Angeles would be apt to experience. Estimates of the working population of Los Angeles directly or indirectly dependent on some phase of defense-procurement industry run as high as 50 per cent.

The trained and disciplined minds that were able to plan, and manage the infinitely complex and difficult tasks of building the Polaris missile system or of putting a man into orbit, or of developing nuclear weapons themselves, could well be directed into the kind of massive undertaking that the engineering, redesigning and rebuilding of a great city would represent.

Some of the cathedrals of Western Europe took a century to design and construct. Perhaps the planning and reconstruction of a great American city designed for people rather than automobiles would take years. It would be infinitely difficult, and have enormous complications politically and socially, but would it not be worth it?

Are we going to be content to plan piecemeal—to clear away a few blocks of downtown blight in order to put up some tall buildings and call it urban renewal? Are we going to abandon the idea of walking to and from neighborhoods and communities, in favor of continuing the endless miles of ribboning concrete-and-steel freeways? Is it too late to ensure that workers may live within a few minutes of the place in which they work, that their

children can walk to schools, libraries, and playgrounds in safety; that there will be parks and
open space available to all who want to use them;
that the air will be clean and pure and healthy and
the water fit for swimming and drinking?

The truth is that our cities are underengineered
and underplanned. We have lost much of the pleas-
ure and vitality of living in natural neighborhoods. We tend to live separate lives, even within
our own families, because of the sheer, brute problems of getting from place to place, and the problem of too many people trying to live together in
cities that were laid out along the designs of a
Roman camp of two thousand years ago.

What is required is a breadth of political vision
and social planning that can conceive of urban
America as beautiful as well as efficient, challeng-
ing and stimulating as well as clean—a nation of
wide diversity of taste, as well as a united one.

What a challenge to our creativity as a society!
We can undertake such a program with the help
of a large variety of specialists who have the
dimension and capacity to challenge current con-
cerns. We will need the help of the city-planners,
the social scientists, the business community, the
artists, the philosophers. A whole series of problems are deeply interrelated, and to maximize the
usefulness of the solutions, the problems must
be approached as a group. If the goal is a re-
structuring of our urban life, we can at the
same time look for solutions to all the problems

which are bred by our current negligence. The problems of air and water pollution, education, conservation, housing, transport, and communications all hinge on our current urban practices. To resolve problems of such magnitude, and in order to hold onto the many advantageous aspects of our lives and society and, at the same time, remove the difficulties, requires social decisions, demanding all our imagination and wisdom.

5 / *Rural Poverty*

One of the great paradoxes of our time is that the envy of the world, American agriculture, is in deep trouble. Having developed a high degree of efficiency, working harder and longer and more diligently than most Americans, the farmer today is denied a reasonable return for his investment of capital, time, and energy. The price of the family farmer's product, and thus the price of his labor and initiative, has fallen far below parity—or a fair income as compared with the rest of the population.

Even the most mechanized and scientific farm families can be hit by disastrous crop failures or catastrophic price declines for their product.

And while the nation struggles to find a way to permit the efficient family farmer to earn a reasonable return in comparison with the non-farm population, an almost-forgotten segment of our rural population lives in real poverty—tenant farmers, sharecroppers, farm laborers, migratory workers, and the farm owners of too-small and inefficient units.

Three-fifths of the farms in the United States produce only about one-eighth of the commodities for market. These farms can, in effect, be called non-commercial. Even the boom prices of the forties did little for the families who operate such farms. The fact is that the rural areas of the United States contain some of the worst slum conditions in America today.

For the most part on farms with thin soil, with relatively poor transportation available, farmers living in poverty are scattered throughout the Appalachian area, the southern Piedmont and Coastal Plains, the hilly regions of the Southeast, in the Ozarks, and in the Mississippi Delta. Where the great stands of timber once ranged throughout the upper Great Lakes area and the West, farm families are still trying to eke out a living in the cut-over areas. And it is probable that most counties in every state have at least a pocket of rural poverty.

In 1960, more than one in three (about 36 per cent) farm families had net incomes below $2,000. These farm families make up 21 per cent of the nation's low-income families.

Poverty is about three times as great in rural areas as it is for the rest of the people of the United States. While Negro farmers, sharecroppers, and farm workers live in desperately poor circumstances in general, 75 per cent of the rural low-income people are white. The children of such families with seriously low income are often denied even a basic education. Studies indicate that about half the children of such families fail to complete even the eighth grade.

Consistently low incomes have driven such farm families to the cities in recent years. The number of farms has dropped steadily as small farmers have quit, sold out, and gone to look for jobs in the cities. Three hundred fifty-nine farmers a day are leaving the farm for the cities. We are losing an average of about 130,000 farmers to the cities every year.

Number of farms by value of farm products sold, United States, selected years, 1939–59

(Thousands of farms)

Value of farm products sold	Number of farms				
	1939	1944	1949	1954	1959
$10,000 or more	312	438	484	583	794
$5,000 to $9,999	585	723	721	707	654
$2,500 to $4,999	1,015	976	882	812	618
Less than $2,500	4,185	3,722	3,292	2,681	1,638
Total	6,097	5,859	5,379	4,783	3,704

There are still, however, too many people in the farm areas for the available work. Agricultural techniques, commercial fertilizer, hybrid seed, and mechanization have so improved efficiency of production that one American farmer today can raise enough to feed twenty-seven people, where fifty years ago his grandfather could typically raise only enough to feed nine.

Young people from farm families drift steadily into towns and cities looking for work. The extraordinary capital costs of establishing a new and efficient farm unit make it almost impossible for a young farmer to go into successful farming unless he inherits a good farm. The result is that the general farm population is aging. In any group of farmers, there will likely be many more older men than young farmers.

Yet, the small farmer clings to his land fiercely. He has pride and independence. He loves the land. It has spiritual as well as economic meaning.

Recently, a Bill Mauldin cartoon illustrated a rural hill farmer crouched behind a stone wall holding a shotgun. His family was on the porch of the house. Beside him was a newspaper with the headline, "LBJ DECLARES WAR ON POVERTY." He is saying, "By dam', they'll know they've been in a fight."

No "solution" to the farm problem is acceptable which would, in effect, force the small farmer off his land. On the other hand, for those farmers who feel that the best opportunities for themselves and their families lie in non-agricultural pursuits, we should step up vocational training and greatly improve educational opportunity.

We should make a strenuous effort to induce

more job-producing industries to locate in rural areas. Many rural families should be able to supplement farm income while remaining on their small farms.

Rural and urban America alike will benefit if we can stem the migration of ill-prepared rural families to the cities. Too many rural communities are becoming ghost towns, for when the farmer-customers leave, business must follow. No matter how efficient a businessman may be, someone must buy his merchandise. A double burden is placed on those who remain—to support the schools and churches, and the other institutions of community life.

In many rural low income areas, the educational level is so low that many do not have the faintest knowledge of how to break out of their traditional cycle of poverty. From father to son, from mother to daughter, poverty and indifference to poverty can be passed from one generation to the next. Special educational efforts are required in these areas.

One of the more successful experiments in American history has been the school lunch program. Yet, for technical reasons, many children are still deprived of the health-giving foods made available through the program. In many instances this is simply due to lack of kitchen facilities at the school. For those areas unable to finance the construction of such facilities in the schools, the Federal government should finance 90 per cent of the cost of construction of such kitchen facilities. Not one child should be denied the benefits of the school lunch program because of lack of facilities.

Congress has provided new and important tools for use in revitalizing the countryside, through the Rural Area Development Program.

Under the Food and Agricultural Act of 1962 the Department of Agriculture was given authority to aid rural people in new long-range programs for putting land not needed for crops into new and profitable uses through "Resource Conservation and Development Projects" and "Rural Renewal Projects."

The Department of Agriculture now can enter into ten-year cost-sharing agreements with farmers and ranchers to carry out long-range conservation plans. Technical help is provided to make changes in cropping systems and land use, and to develop soil, forest, wildlife, and recreation resources. State and local public agencies designated by the governor or the state legislature to carry out land-use plans can be given thirty-year federal loans.

Rural Renewal Projects, in severely disadvantaged areas where much of the land is not being put to its best use, can help create conditions that will make these communities more attractive to private investment. Resource Conservation and Development projects also can be locally initiated and locally sponsored to provide a framework for stepped-up programs of conservation, development, and use of all land, water, and related resources.

Under new amendments to the law, the Department of Agriculture can pay up to 30 per cent of the total cost of a reservoir to store water for future municipal and industrial use, with deferred repayment and interest charges. Reservoirs or other areas of public recreation can now be financed by cost-sharing and long-term loans to state and local agencies. And for the first time, the Farmers Home Administration can now make forty-year, low-interest loans to individual farmers for development of outdoor recreation. The owner-operator of a family-size farm may borrow up to $60,000 for construction of fish ponds, development of hunting preserves, construction of cabins, picnic, and camping areas, and other facilities for outdoor recreation.

We are indeed short of outdoor recreational opportunities for the vast majority of employed workers. The pressures on the available camping and fishing areas near centers of population is tremendous. We need now many more summer camps for children, more parks and campsites. Here is an opportunity to kill two birds with one stone—to provide healthful recreation for the city dwellers and to step up income for those who wish to remain in the rural areas.

Parts of the Iron Range-Upper Peninsula and

the Appalachian regions, for example, clearly should be developed as recreational areas for our rapidly growing population.

In the all-out attack on rural poverty we must enlist the farm co-operatives. In fact, any program designed to help farm families should encourage and promote the development of co-operatives. (Existing co-operatives might well take on additional tasks, specifically directed toward providing services, supplies, and facilities not now available to low-income families, and possibly also serving as a market place for their products.) The Bank for Co-operatives might well extend government-guaranteed loans at low interest to set up new enterprises managed by the experienced co-operatives for the benefit of low-income farmers.

Other loans and advisory programs should be utilized to help small poverty-stricken farmers to expand their operations—loans large enough to enable them to get a fresh start, and with repayment terms liberal enough so that farmers have a reasonable chance of repayment. Of course, there should be a reasonable prospect of success, otherwise we may be doing more harm than good.

A primary tool for the redevelopment and revitalization of a rural area enlists businessmen and farmers in a joint planning operation—the industrial development corporation. In some rural areas, a local community has undertaken such planning. In others, whole multi-county areas have been looked at as a single entity, as in the case of the recently established Northeastern Minnesota Development Association.

In every case, the secret is local initiative and planning coupled with governmental funds and technical assistance.

One such program began nine years ago in Ava, Missouri, with the establishment of an industrial development corporation. By 1959, in four years, the tide of migration and declining income in Ava had reversed and an upward trend had begun. Today annual business activity is more than 1 million dollars higher than it was in 1955, 120 new homes have been built, and real estate values have increased 20 per cent. Two new industries providing 285 jobs are in operation, and a third plant costing a quarter-million dollars is under construction. New community facilities and recreation areas have been developed, and agricultural marketing operations have improved. The interaction of private initiative and governmental encouragement was important.

The Ava industrial committee had little trouble raising $24,000 to buy land for an industrial park, but it took the state's promise to build a highway before the committee could get a sporting goods manufacturer to announce he would locate in Ava.

More than 1,200 people bought the initial stock in the Ava Industrial Development Corporation to build a factory to house the firm. With the help of a $125,000 Federal Area Redevelopment Administration loan, the plant was enlarged in 1962.

Now the parent company of the sporting goods manufacturer is building a $260,000 plant of its own in the industrial park.

The industrial committee also got a wood-treatment plant to locate in Ava. The wood plant is now expanding to double its output. The plant, originally financed jointly by a local bank and the Small Business Administration, employs fifty people at present.

The Ava Industrial Development Corporation spearheaded other local developments. It stimulated feeder pig and feeder cattle producing and marketing programs that have more than doubled income from these two sources. It initiated an annual eight-day Glade Top Trail guided tour which attracted some 6,000 people from twenty-two states its first year. In 1963, it persuaded the Forestry Service to improve the Glade Top Trail area, using Federal Accelerated Public Works funds. A special lighting system was designed to encourage tourists to drive through Ava rather than taking a bypass. With state help, a roadside park was developed and 110 acres of land bought and set aside for future recreational use.

With the stimulation of such local leadership, Ava has been converted to a dial telephone system, and the telephone company persuaded to extend its service to 500 farms. A $350,000 high school and a new jail have been built, the latter financed in part with the Accelerated Public Works funds. Permanent concrete bleachers and night lighting were installed in the local ballpark. The city's water and sewage systems also have been expanded.

All in all, the case of Ava, Missouri, demonstrates the effectiveness of concentrating on the expansion of local urban industrial employment as one important solution to agriculture's low-income problem.

In distressed rural areas in general, the availability of nearby jobs and the ease of getting to and from employment centers are more important than the farm income itself in determining who will leave the farm or stay.

In those areas of the Southeast, for example, in which farm people have made the greatest economic gains, they have generally been located in close proximity to developing urban industrial centers. Most of the counties of the Southeast which have caught up with the national average in living levels either include or are located in close proximity to such centers.

While there have been rapid declines in farm employment in such areas, there has also tended to be a rise in output and income per farm worker and per farm family. The pressure of underemployment on the nearby farms has been lifted by the job opportunities in the new nearby industrial developments.

Technical and managerial assistance to those low-income farmers who have the managerial ability, and who can put together enough land and machinery to make a shift from low-income to commercial agriculture, should be a prime objective.

Farm machinery is costly. Big tractors run $32,000, a mechanical plow $7,000, but machinery is needed to expand a farmer's productivity. Advances in fertilizing and crop dusting are amazing, but they all require capital and sufficient acreage to make them pay off.

Competing alone, the small farming units are underproductive, with a high unit cost of production. Today, for example, it costs $61 an acre to grow corn on a 160-acre farm, compared with $54 on a 640-acre farm. The smaller farms cannot compete with mechanization successfully, and without available credit farmers cannot afford the high cost of modern equipment.

The farm co-operative principle should be expanded in such areas. The low yield and high costs confronting small landowners can often be reduced if they can be helped to pool their purchasing and marketing activities. This amalgamation would apply even where a conversion to recreational facilities or other land usage is taking place.

In most areas, it is impossible to enlarge existing farms to an efficient size without at the same time reducing the number of farms. But the combination of non-farm jobs nearby for some farm operators, and the availability of credit to buy up the farms of such ex-farmers can permit the building up of family farms of a size that can sustain a commercial farming operation, or of co-operative producing units made up of smaller farmers.

In the effort to raise the level of rural living we must not overlook the 2 million men, women, and children who work for wages on the farms of the United States. About two-thirds of all farm workers in 1959 earned less than $1,000 annually in money wages, including not only their earnings from farm work, but also their earnings from non-farm work. The total number of days worked per year was shockingly low. The average annual money wages were only $1,025 for a man and $447 for a woman migratory worker, and only $1,278 for a man and $314 for a woman non-migratory worker.

Part-time farm workers (migratory or non-migratory), particularly Negro farm workers in the South, are probably the most depressed group of people in the country. Automation has not come to the business of picking fruits and vegetables. Usually this backbreaking work is done by hand, and this work does not pay well.

Migratory farm laborers can be found throughout the southern part of the country, particularly in Florida, Texas, Arizona, New Mexico, and California, where most fruits and vegetables are grown. Some of the conditions described by John Steinbeck's *The Grapes of Wrath* are still with us. In most cases the migrant workers are unorganized. There is no bargaining for wages or working conditions. They take what they can get—when they can get it.

Non-migrant workers differ in their conditions only in that they stay put between harvests. Their working conditions are approximately the same.

Florida, for example, has a large number of migrant workers. According to the Florida State Employment Service, most harvesting in the state pays $7 for a nine-hour day, about 80¢ an hour. Celery cutting, which is harder work, pays an average of $1.01 an hour. These are not high wages; more troublesome is the fact that work is very spotty. Many days, there is no work at all. Frequently, only a few hours of work are available.

The Department of Agriculture, the Extension Service and its County Agents, along with the Department of Labor should do much more to help the migrant agricultural workers receive better wages and working conditions. For example, with the help of the Federal Fish and Wildlife Service the sardine industry has established better and more stabilized wages. The sardine industry has historically been an uncertain one. The catch is variable and the fish run at variable times. Because of these fluctuations, the workers had to take what they could get whenever they could get it. Now the fisheries and canners are getting a better quality of work.

We must bring to migrant workers the protection of existing labor and social legislation, extending coverage of the minimum wage law and social security. For migrant labor we must provide assurance of a comprehensive program to bring them not only decent wages, but also adequate standards of health, housing, social security protection, and education and welfare services. Certainly a great step forward would be a federal contribution toward the establishment of housing facilities for migrant workers, perhaps the worst-housed of all Americans.

One of the reasons migrant and non-migrant farm laborers are in such an unfavorable position is that the growers of fruits and vegetables, either individuals or companies, are themselves faced with an uncertain market. Prices often fluctuate from week to week. Bad weather may wipe out a season's crop in a matter of minutes, putting considerable pressure on the grower.

There has been a trend to stabilize this market on the part of many buyers, by contracting their purchases in advance. This has a tendency to reduce the hazards confronting the growers. If the market becomes less hazardous for the growers, the atmosphere for better wages and working conditions will improve substantially. Government should investigate every means possible to improve the marketing position of growers, including the expanded use of Marketing Agreements and Orders, marketing associations and cooperatives.

Programs to promote overseas export of foods and fibers to underdeveloped countries should be pushed even more aggressively; better nutrition programs for our own low-income population should similarly be advanced. These and improved educational standards in rural areas should help all farmers.

The farmer has served the consuming public of America well. Most Americans are the best-fed people in the world. Yet to maintain this high standard we pay only 18.8 per cent of what we earn for food. The British pay 29.5 per cent, the Italians 44.7 per cent, and the Russians 53 per cent of their earnings for food.

Farm labor is not the major factor in the cost of food to the housewife. From every dollar the housewife spends at the grocery store, the farmer gets 37¢, compared with 52¢ some years back. Farm labor is only a fraction of that 37¢, which also includes seed, planting, fertilizers, boxing, machinery, and all other out-of-pocket costs to the farmer as well.

Food is one of the better values on the market today. Item by item, its price has increased less over the years than virtually any other category of consumer purchases. Little of this small increase accrued to the farmer, but went to the other services involved, including freight, packaging, distribution, and wholesale and retail mark-ups.

Just as farm labor represents a small percentage of the end cost of food, food commodities themselves frequently constitute only a small fraction of the price the housewife pays at the store. Her loaf of bread, for example, which costs her about 22¢, includes only about 2¢ worth of wheat.

Those who own farms and those who work on them deserve better of their fellow Americans. Cheap food and cheap fiber to the factories and consumers must ultimately be paid for by the poverty of the rural population. A fair price for the farmer's and farm worker's labor should continue to be a prime objective, as we also move forward on specific programs of the kind we have discussed in this chapter.

Finally, the solution to the plight of the small farmer cannot be found within agriculture alone. A higher rate of general economic growth—providing more non-farm job opportunities in and near rural communities—will have a decided and favorable impact on the problem of poverty in the rural areas.

6 / *The Depressed Areas:*
Why Abandon Success?

Ten or fifteen years ago the regional development of the Columbia River and public power were the hottest political issues in the Northwest. The question of whether private or public power interests should build a multipurpose dam or dams at Hell's Canyon was debated at almost every meeting from the Lions Club in Portland to the Farmers Grange in Boise.

Political careers during 1948 through 1956 were made or broken depending on whether the candidate or office-holder was for or against Hell's Canyon or the Columbia Valley Authority. When the debate started in Oregon the Republican opponents of regional development had both Senate seats and the majority of seats in the House. When the smoke cleared, the Democrats, who had favored regional development and public power had both Senate seats, as well as a majority of the seats in the House.

The same trend could be seen in Washington, Idaho, western Montana and northern California.

What might be called the concept of the valley authority was founded on the idea that there existed in some parts of the country homogeneous areas that depended on basic natural resources for prosperity. Thirty years ago this idea was usually based on a natural resource such as a river or a water system with hydro-electric potential.

The river systems of the Columbia, the Tennessee, the Missouri, and the St. Lawrence dividing Canada and our Northeastern states were in some respects as much an evil as a potential blessing. They would flood during seasonal rains; navigation was hazardous as the silt clogged channels and changed directions. The water, ever flowing downstream, and the swollen tributaries eroded land and washed off fertile topsoil into the Atlantic, the Gulf of Mexico, or the Pacific.

The establishment of the Tennessee Valley Authority, the best known and most successful regional development program in America, changed this and established a new regional concept.

I have never been able to understand why we failed to carry on equivalent regional rehabilitation elsewhere. One has only to drive through TVA territory to know what regional thinking and the encouragement of a joint effort between government and private enterprise can accomplish. TVA country is lush, green, and prosperous.

When you leave the TVA region you cross over into the wasteland of Appalachia.

TVA came into being in 1933, at the end of the Great Depression and the beginning of the New Deal.

The following thirty years saw tremendous growth and accomplishment in navigation, flood control, power development and distribution, development of new and better fertilizers, agricultural and forest development, erosion control and reforestation, and other phases of resource use.

Development of the river has been teamed with protection and development of the watershed. Encouraging full use of resources, the people of the region have found much greater scope for their initiative, energy, and talents. Both the Tennessee Valley and the nation as a whole have been strengthened.

The federal investment in TVA has paid off many times over.

More than 311,000 rural people, nearly a quarter of a million of them farmers, got electric service for the first time. By 1950, four-fifths of the region's farmers had service, compared with a fourth in 1945 and one-twenty-eighth back in 1933. For the small farmer, TVA has meant irrigation and an effective and profitable infrastructure.

TVA flood control proved itself in 1946, 1947, and 1948 by clipping 10 to 12½ feet from the fifth-, sixth-, and seventh-largest floods of record in the area, saving millions of dollars in damage for privately owned farms and other property.

Traffic on the new waterway doubled in the first five years and after 1950 nearly tripled, reaching 1.5 billion ton-miles. The now navigable waters became a strong inducement to industrial development and by 1963, some 875 million dollars of private capital had been invested in waterfront plants and terminals. The value of recreational facilities on and along the lakes passed 150 million dollars.

The concept of TVA has been hotly argued elsewhere—but not in Tennessee. Right or left, the people of Tennessee know what TVA has accomplished.

On May 18, 1963, President Kennedy spoke before a crowd of 15,000 people at Muscle Shoals, Alabama, commemorating the thirtieth year of TVA. He said: ". . . the work of TVA will never be over. There will always be new frontiers for it to conquer. For in the minds of men the world over, the initials TVA stand for progress. . . ."

The underlying principle on which the TVA operates is that there is a unity and interrelationship in a region's resources. The fullest and most effective use of resources can be achieved when they are developed in a unified or integrated program. The TVA program extends to the improvement of the forest and agricultural lands of the region, the watershed, as well as to the development of the river system itself through dams and reservoirs.

The figures for 1962 alone are impressive. In that year, twenty-seven new forest-products industries began operating in the 200-county Tennessee Valley region, comprised of counties in the Valley proper plus counties outside the Valley where TVA power is distributed. In addition, thirty-five existing plants announced expansion plans. The new plants and expansions represented an estimated $5,676,000 in investment and more than 3,000 new jobs.

In spite of this remarkable record, the political fight for regional development programs seems to have vanished.

The Area Redevelopment Administration bill which to some extent applies regional thinking was the first major piece of legislation John F. Kennedy signed after becoming President in 1961. It looked ahead the expenditure of 375 million dollars to stimulate economic activity and to build needed public facilities in areas of high, chronic unemployment. Most of the funds (300 million dollars) were to be devoted to long-term loans, and the balance to be distributed to the communities in the form of grants.

By the end of 1963, the agency had committed a little over 200 million dollars. It says that these funds have helped create some 20,000 new jobs and will eventually expand employment in distressed areas by 60,000.

The ARA has designated over 1,000 areas as "depressed" and therefore eligible for redevelopment assistance; these include about a fifth of the entire population of the country. This has caused a dilution of the program. It is valiantly trying to do too much for too many with too little.

Of all the depressed areas, Appalachia has become the best known. A look at what has happened here will serve as a guide-line elsewhere.

Generally, depressed areas differ from the Tennessee Valley in that these regions are not centered around a single resource yet to be harnessed, such as a river. But, and this is most important, the theory behind regional rehabilitation and effective infrastructure is applicable in both cases. The depressed areas generally depended on a productive resource that has become obsolete or worked out or too costly to compete any longer. Frequently this has been an extractive product—an ore or mineral.

In Appalachia it was coal. Not only was the use of coal cut back sharply, the simultaneous introduction of new machines to mine coal greatly reduced manpower requirements and also further aggravated the drop in regional income from coal.

The economy of the area has been further hampered by a series of serious floods. What little income was left was largely drained away by absentee owners.

As a result, the per capita income in Appalachia is only three-quarters what it is in the rest of the United States, and 7 to 8 per cent of the labor force is unemployed. In the last decade, total employment has declined when, by contrast, there has been a nation-wide increase of 15 per cent.

All of this has depressed the tax base in Appalachia. Property here has an assessed per capita valuation of 38 per cent less than the national average. Education and all other community services in the area have suffered. There are 23 per cent fewer high-school graduates on the average in Appalachia than in the rest of the country.

An idea of what this kind of depression does to the so-called multiplier factor is shown by the fact that had the people of Appalachia purchased retail goods on the national average, an additional 4 billion dollars in goods would have been sold in the area per annum. People in the rest of the United States generally spend about twice as much for services as do the poor people of Appalachia.

This kind of depressed area is a costly drag on the economy. The total *monthly* Federal expenditure in Appalachia for welfare alone—including food programs, but excluding unemployment compensation and social security—is at least *41 million dollars*. In one year this amounts to 500 million dollars; in ten to almost 5 billion dollars. That is a lot of money.

Appalachia does have natural resources. It contains some of the nation's richest mineral deposits, a good annual rainfall, and fine timber stands.

Appalachia cuts across ten states from Pennsylvania to Alabama, and includes an area about ten times the size of Switzerland. Over 15 million people live here.

It will not do to abandon this region and say to its 15 million people, "If you don't like it, move." Nor can we just continue massive welfare payments to Appalachia indefinitely. We must do something better.

President Kennedy appointed a Regional Commission to study the problems of Appalachia. Its report, filed in the Spring of 1964, stressed the need for regional development saying:

The major objective of this regional development process is clear: Appalachia must attain an employment base which can sustain its people at a level of dignity and prosperity comparable to the relatively affluent nation of which it is part. The conversion and processing of its raw materials should be done locally to the fullest extent possible. New industries, dependent not only on the resources of the region but on the strategic location and potential market which Appalachia represents, must be located in the region. The magnificent recreational resources must be developed with co-ordinated intensity if their employment potential is to be realized. Agricultural diversification should be accelerated and mining and timber employment and income expanded.

Private enterprise will be the ultimate employer.

The difficulties facing a region of desperate poverty like Appalachia can be overcome if only we will think and plan on a sufficiently large scale. We have already mounted small attacks even within Appalachia by utilizing a smaller-scale joint venture arrangement and the kind of leverage government can provide.

There is for example a small city in Appalachia named Hazleton, Pennsylvania.

The people of Hazleton, together with the Federal government, set up the kind of joint venture I have been describing. They have proved that we can do something about hoisting ourselves out of poverty and unemployment if we will exercise our initiative and will.

Hazleton, like many a community in Appalachia, was dependent on coal mining. In 1956, the mines were flooded by Hurricane Diana. This was the death blow to an economy that had been collapsing for thirty years.

Overnight, half of the work force was unemployed. People began to leave Hazleton at the rate of 1,000 a year. Hazleton was on the verge of becoming another derelict ghost town.

The people of Hazleton did not sit back and wring their hands. They rolled up their sleeves and went to work. With help from the Federal government, they formed a local company named CAN DO. CAN DO are the initials for Community Area New Development Organization. They raised over 2 million dollars from the local utility companies, banks, and stores, as well as from the sale of fifteen-year 3 per cent debenture bonds. With this money, CAN DO planned an industrial park. They brought fifteen new industries into town. They created 4,000 new jobs. Unemployment is down from 50 to 8.5 per cent.

Today in Hazleton there is a new foam rubber factory, metal fabrication plants, an immense bakery, and a plant for highway trailers. There is a plastic wood company operated by Japanese. Hazleton knew that for every basic new production job something like five service jobs are also created. There is hair to be cut, laundry to be washed, cars to be oiled and greased.

Not every town or city or slum, or impoverished rural area can become a Hazleton overnight, but Hazleton demonstrates that our leaders of business, finance, education, and labor, working in partnership with government, can quickly go far to fulfill the promise of America.

Federal help to Appalachia has begun. ARA has allocated about one-third of its funds to this one area while accelerated public-works funds expended almost a quarter of its total here. It has not been enough.

The President's Commission recommended a series of federal expenditures over a five-year period. The basic effect would be to rebuild the area's infrastructure, and put Appalachia on the way back.

The cost of this effort for the first year—which the Commission calls a "heavy commitment of Federal funds" will be about 230 million dollars. *This is less than half of what we are today spending in welfare payments in Appalachia.*

To me this kind of approach—a regional approach, where the Federal government acts as the stimulus for new industry and new jobs so that these areas can stand on their own feet—makes good sense. It is also cheaper in the long run.

I want to see the concept of regional rehabilitation and planning greatly enlarged. All that is required is some forward thinking and a little initiative.

I have never understood why it is perfectly proper for a family to plan ahead or for a business to look to the future but not for a government. I doubt if a corporate executive in today's economy would last through the next stockholders' meeting unless he was able to show the owners of the business constructive thinking for the years to come. The citizens of this country stand in the same relation to the government as stockholders to their company. They own the business. It is their government; they pay the expenses for running it; they pay the salaries of the executives who make the decisions. Instead of scoffing at planning the people ought to demand it. The elected officials of the country should be required to show plans for the future.

If we are to undertake to rehabilitate these

areas; if we are to stop paying astronomical sums in welfare; if we are to give them a productive, full-scale role in the economy of the nation—our approach must be one of long-range regional planning.

The Tennessee Valley was once a blighted region. It is a shining example of how the Federal government can join with the private sector in creating a planned and designed regional economy with consequent benefit for all. We must not turn our back on a successful experiment as we have done in the case of TVA. Rather, we should work to improve on the model.

7 / Civil Rights and Poverty

The issues of poverty and civil rights are deeply intertwined, presenting the central moral problem of our time. Although it is true that three-quarters of the poor are white, it is a tragic fact that half the non-whites are poor.

The statistics of poverty bear witness to the results of years of discrimination and apathy on the part of the white majority.

In 1962, the average white man's family income was $5,642; the Negro's $3,023; the Indian's $1,500; poorest of all are the Americans of Mexican extraction, who, according to 1960 census figures, did not fit into a single classification in which their average family income even approximated the $3,000 cut-off point.

The 1960 census showed that 3.6 million Negro men were employed. Forty per cent of all the jobs held by Negroes were in heavy-duty and low paying occupations such as laborers (1 million), janitors, porters, cooks, and elevator operators (½ million).

Contrary to the widely held belief that Indians receive some sort of consistent dole from the Federal government, they are as dependent on the general economy to provide opportunity and jobs as the rest of the population. Often unable to gain acceptance in the general community, they tend to stay on the reservations which cannot provide more than minimal employment at low levels. Forty to fifty per cent, seven to eight times the national average, are unemployed.

Job opportunities for Mexican-Americans, a group of citizens whose plight is so little-known that even census figures are unreliable, was dramatized in the fall of 1963 by Congressman Henry B. Gonzales in testimony taken by a sub-committee of the Senate Labor Committee.

Commenting upon his experiences as a member of the Texas State Senate, he said:

. . . this case came to my attention. A young lady of Latin extraction held a clerical position at a local library. She had none of the cultural traits associated with Latins: she spoke no Spanish, and was highly skilled and well-educated. Yet this girl was paid $25 per month less than her co-workers doing the same job. Her employer explained, "the other girls would quit if I paid her as much as they make." This example of wage discrimination in a public agency shows ample evidence of wage discrimination in all areas of the Texas economy.

Of the approximately 4.5 million Americans of
Mexican extraction, almost one-quarter become
migrant workers, following the harvest from state
to state. These migrants, lacking a fixed place of
residence and employment, do not come under the
protection of Federal laws and are therefore in-
eligible for any sort of public assistance. On the
average they work no more than 131 days a year
often earning less than 50 cents an hour. Those
taking jobs as laundry workers often earn less
than $15 for a forty-four- to forty-eight-hour week.
Again, racial discrimination and the absence of
coverage under minimum wage and hour laws and
Fair Employment Practice Laws remove any
chance of a change in the present status of these
agricultural migrants.

Figures contrasting equivalent jobs held by
whites and Negroes are equally startling. For example, about one-fourth of all semi-skilled Negroes
are truck drivers or deliverymen who earn on the
average $2,600 a year. The average for white truck
drivers is $4,500.

Even on a higher economic level, with jobs demanding skill and experience, the Negro now fails
to achieve similar pay scales.

Perhaps the most deplorable statistic and one
indicative of Negro unrest is that a Negro who has
completed four years of college will earn less in his
lifetime than a white man with far less schooling.

Dr. Herman Miller of the Census Bureau points

out in his book, *Rich Man, Poor Man,* that even in Federal government the Negro does not stand on equal footing. On examining hiring figures he states:

The concentration of Negroes in the lower-paid jobs that was so evident in the figures for the country as a whole also appears in Federal employment statistics. Not only are Negroes disproportionately represented in the lower-paid manual and clerical Federal jobs, but they are barely represented at all in the middle and upper echelons of government service.

The many books and magazine articles commenting on the progress of the non-white over the past few years makes for encouraging reading, but in reality the relative position of the Negro, at least in regard to income, has grown worse. Dr. Miller points out that:

. . . most of the improvement in the occupational status of the Negro since 1940 has been due to his movement from the rural South to the urban industrial areas rather than to any major improvement in job opportunities. . . . The results show that there have been few significant changes in the occupational distribution of non-white males relative to whites during the past twenty years.

Non-whites are discriminated against in education, in job opportunities, in housing, in health services, in every way. No matter how rich in economic terms the non-white may be, he experiences a continual and almost total exclusion from white society. This lack of acceptance pervades his entire existence and influences his every action. Even when he has the ability to pay, the non-white finds it difficult to obtain decent living conditions.

Before me is a guidebook called "Touring with Towser" distributed by the American Automobile Association. It lists hundreds of places of public accommodation that will take guests with dogs. Now let us consider the problems facing a Negro family looking forward to a trip. How many places of public accommodation can they go to where they can obtain a room without fear of being humiliated by racial discrimination? The comparison is heartbreaking.

For example, in Augusta, Georgia, there are five hotels and motels that will take dogs, and only one where a Negro can go with confidence. In Columbus, Georgia, there are six places for dogs and none for Negroes. In Charleston, South Carolina, there are ten places where a dog can stay, none for a Negro.

Information available on 275 cities with populations of over ten thousand in the eleven states of the South and in the border states of Kentucky, Maryland, Oklahoma, and West Virginia show that 60 per cent of the restaurants and theaters and 43 per cent of the lunch counters are segregated. In the same states, in cities having a population of less than ten thousand, the figures climb to between 85 and 90 per cent.

It has been over ten years since the Supreme Court held it unconstitutional to maintain racial segregation in public schools. The sad fact is that despite a welter of litigation three states—Alabama, Mississippi, and South Carolina—do not have a single Negro child registered in a white school below the college level. In the eleven Southern states, ten years of laws suits have produced a 1 per cent rate of school desegregation. At this rate, taking into account the fact that there are nearly two thousand bi-racial school districts, the Supreme Court's mandate will not be a reality for centuries.

Stewart Alsop has pointed out that in a few years there will be non-white majorities in many of our major cities. The nation can no longer tolerate conditions where certain members of its citizens are merely kept in school to pass away the time until they are old enough to enter the labor market —completely unprepared to take their place in a highly specialized society. How can a Negro family provide educational stimuli for its children when they see that even with the benefit of an education, there is little opportunity for a job commensurate with the level of education achieved by the child?

In the face of continued segregation and discrimination is it any wonder that the Negroes demonstrate for their rights? Is it necessary for us to undergo further decades of violence and tension before the Negro becomes a full citizen? To my mind, the patience of the Negro is amazing.

To stamp out discrimination in this country we must use every weapon possible. Pressure for equal educational opportunities through legislation must continue. Observance of the provisions of the Civil Rights Bill, particularly those sections eliminating discrimination in public accommodations and Fair Employment Practices, must be the concern of every citizen.

During my administration as mayor of Minneapolis, we persuaded the Board of Aldermen to pass the country's first FEPC ordinance. We learned, however, that passing a law prohibiting discriminatory employment practices was not enough; we had to get out and convince every element of the city to help enforce the ordinance. The same effort and cooperation is necessary to help insure compliance with the Civil Rights Bill.

We often hear the argument that you cannot legislate morality, yet we do enact a variety of laws dealing with immoral acts. Every state has legislation against robbery, arson, extortion and other crimes against individuals and society. It requires more than law to put an end to racial prejudice. The law only expresses the determination not to accept discrimination and to use legal means to abolish it. To be effective the realization of the law must find expression in the minds and hearts of men. The 25 states which have fair employment legislation at present have found that the laws have worked and caused no meaningful disruptions of business or private rights. No state which has passed such legislation has had cause to repeal it. Passage of the Civil Rights Bill will not eliminate all the evils of racial prejudice, but it will set down a legal framework for constructive social policy that is long overdue.

Discrimination costs this country between thirteen and seventeen million dollars every year in revenue and production. This is more than a fourth of the money we spend for national defense and three times as much as we spend on our space program.

This loss in income does not take into account the incalculable costs we pay in higher crime rates, poor health, urban decay, mounting welfare costs and the countless other indirect costs that flow from discriminatory practices.

We can do something about these problems and a key step has been achieved by Mr. Eugene Foley, of the Small Business Administration.

The SBA has initiated training programs in Washington, Philadelphia and New York, for Negro businessmen in order that they may qualify for loans from the Small Business Administration. In addition, Mr. Foley has approved the establishment of a Small Business Investment Corporation in Harlem which is expected to make selected investments in local business. By stimulating a class of small business owners, it is hoped that the entire neighborhood will benefit from the increase in capital improvements.

The same effort must be made to assist Indians and Mexican-Americans to raise their standard of living. Although suffering from discrimination, the Mexican-Americans have an additional problem due to the fact that many do not speak or understand English. It is essential that a combined program of vocational training and language communication be instituted at once so that they can achieve the necessary skills to take advantage of job training programs that will enable them to take roots in a community.

The problem of raising the standard of living of the Indian is unique in that existing discrimination is compounded by the Indian's traditional attachment to his land. He is bound to his reservation by religious ties, strong family associations and the hereditary inculcation that land is an essential of life—not to be bought and sold, but to be passed on from father to son.

During the last fifteen years, the Federal government made a determined attempt to relocate Indians in major urban areas. Experience proved that taking a man with few marketable skills into a highly industrial area was both a financial and psychological disaster. Unable to compete in the marketplace, the Indian was not equipped by experience to improve his educational and economic well-being and as a result drifted back to the reservation. The federal attempt resulted in a mere transfer of the problem.

An Indian relocation program should employ far more sustained follow-through, more intensive training, more direct support until the Indian worker and his family can take root in a new community.

For the Indians who have been trained in skills that are marketable in the cities, the cooperation of business and labor with the Indian Bureau in finding jobs is imperative.

Similar efforts concentrating on helping specific and wholly voluntary relocations of Indian workers from the reservation to the cities should be expanded.

Under the sensitive direction of Commissioner Philleo Nash, the Bureau of Indian Affairs is now helping Indian workers by providing both transportation and subsistence for the job seeker and his immediate family, and cooperating with the voluntary organizations in locating jobs for the Indians coming into our urban areas.

While relocation opportunities should be increasingly available, the reservation areas must also be strenuously redeveloped. The answer to improving the economic conditions of the Indian reservations is similar to the requirements necessary to alleviate the poverty in the distressed areas of the hill country of Kentucky and Tennessee, and the coal areas of West Virginia, Pennsylvania and Illinois.

Adequate education is necessary to utilize natural resources located on the reservation area. New opportunities for employment must be brought into the area by industrial and commercial investment as well as tourism.

A great barrier began to swing aside on the day when the Civil Rights bill passed—a barrier that for generations had been damming back tremendous intellectual resources, incalculable energy and vitality lost to the American nation.

I say "began." For if the door is being unlocked, if the door is swinging open, it is only just ajar. There will be no miracle wrought overnight. Rather, then will come the real test of the maturity of our people. The bill itself is but the expression of the determination of the American people to destroy discrimination. The test will be whether colored and white in America can now together— work not only to dissolve the barriers between them, but to develop a healthier and more active sense of community. That task will test the wisdom, the patience, the judgment, and the courage of leaders in both the colored and the white communities.

8 / Disaster Insurance:
The Role of Public Welfare

Contrary to what most people think, less than one-fourth of the families classified as poor receive any public assistance whatsoever.

Most of the poor work—and they work hard.

I have spent most of my life in public service and my experience is that most people on relief are desperately trying to get off the rolls. The stigma of "being on relief" keeps many of those eligible from applying for assistance.

Ours is a country with a conscience and a sense of responsibility. As long as there are human frailties we will have with us the infirm, the handicapped, the retarded, the very young and the old. They cannot support themselves. These people must have help. They are the hard core of the unemployable.

Disaster may strike anyplace. A wage earner may become ill, victimized by some serious disease

that will take him off the payroll for months or
even years. Suppose, for instance, you own a store
in a one-industry town. Your children are going
to private school. You live in one of the large
houses "on the hill." But suddenly a technological change wipes out that one industry, as the
coal industry has been devastated in Appalachia.
Overnight, 5,000 of your customers can be thrown
out of work and have no money to spend—not on
medicines, not at the soda fountain, and not on
cosmetics and toasters.

You have children to educate, a mortgage on
your house, payments to make on the merchandise
for which you no longer have a market. Suddenly,
through no lack of your own energy and ingenuity,
you have no more customers. Your business can be
destroyed.

No matter how successful we may be in our war
against poverty, there will always be the temporarily unemployed. As a business fails, as techniques of production change, as automation and
cybernation strike, as the constant ebb and flow
of our great economy shifts, some people will be
thrown out of work. Anyone of us may be unemployed at some time.

The purpose of the welfare laws is to care for
those who cannot earn a livelihood and to tide over
those temporarily out of work. These laws do not
in themselves cure anything. Their true function
is as an insurance policy against disease for all
elements of society. This is the obligation of those

of us who believe that to some degree we are our brothers' keepers.

These laws came to great prominence during the early years of the Franklin Roosevelt administration. It was the feeling of the people then, as it is today, that all Americans have a right to the essentials of life—decent housing, decent clothing, and something to eat—even when it means the rest of us must subsidize these essentials through taxation or charitable organizations.

There are still those who would let the unemployable, the infirm, and those temporarily out of work fend for themselves. I do not understand this kind of cruelty. I suggest that this attitude is the product of a failure either to understand the facts or a blind refusal to look poverty squarely in the eye.

Before going any further we ought to dispose of the myth that abuses of the palliative devices of the welfare laws are widespread. Studies in recent years have shown only a very small incidence of fraud in public assistance.

Senator Abraham Ribicoff, when he was Secretary of Health, Education and Welfare, said that misunderstanding of these laws is founded on three false assumptions that public assistance is for chiselers; that aid to dependent-children programs causes illegitimacy; that public welfare perpetuates dependency.

As to the charge of chiseling, of a total of 7,225,000 people on public assistance, 5,500,000 were either children, aged, blind, or markedly disabled. Help to children, the elderly and the infirm can hardly be termed chiseling.

As to illegitimacy, Secretary Ribicoff pointed out that only one out of every eight children born out of wedlock was on AFDC (Aid and Services to Families of Dependent Children), and only twenty per cent of children on AFDC rolls were born illegitimately, a figure not substantially higher than the percentage of illegitimacy in low-income groups generally.

Disputing the charge of over-dependency, he points out that newcomers to a community who became eligible for public assistance received it for an average of only one year, and the average length of time it was received by a mother with small children was only two and a quarter years. The idea of people flocking to localities for relief and staying on until their children could raise their own relief-supported families is indeed a myth.

Fortunately, blind attacks against the various welfare programs have had the effect of bringing about a better understanding of our welfare measures and of strengthening them elsewhere.

Public shock and indignation were aroused after Joseph P. Mitchell, the former city manager of Newburgh, New York, announced his highly publicized crackdown on welfare recipients. The same indignation and perhaps some measure of public understanding resulted from the recent cut-off of

AFDC grants to some 23,000 unfortunate children of unwed mothers in Louisiana.

Many people tend to think that the federal welfare statutes constitute a plethora of complex legislation and a vast number of programs calculated to create a socialistic welfare state. Actually they are reasonably simple, and certainly modest.

There are a variety of programs to help people in trouble. Most of these are carried on by the states themselves, under local statutes with matching federal funds.

Many of these programs are included in the Social Security Act of 1935 and subsequent amendments. The more significant are unemployment and old age insurance, Old Age Assistance (OAA), Aid and Services to Families of Dependent Children (AFDC), Aid to the Blind (AB), and Aid to the Permanently and Totally Disabled. The act also covers other public responsibilities such as relief for the destitute, some foster care, and some child welfare services in rural areas.

Anyone who thinks that the relief rolls are jammed with people enjoying a bonanza should be made aware of the facts. In March, 1963, the average cash payment to individuals on AFDC— these are fatherless families where children are involved—was less than $30 *a month*.

Somewhat better off were those receiving Old Age Assistance. But they averaged less than $61 a month. I do not understand how these people get along. It is hard for me to understand how anyone would want to "chisel" his way onto a relief roll for this kind of money.

The categories of poor families receiving public assistance vary from *forty per cent among the disabled to six per cent for the able-bodied self-employed.* In other words, 94 out of 100 of the able-bodied poor were working, and not on welfare.

Generally speaking, the theory behind welfare is that when a job is available any qualified person presently receiving assistance must report for the job. In some cases welfare offices are poorly administered. In others, poor local organization and red tape is to blame. This kind of situation is a failure of administrative detail and should be remedied. But it is not a failure of basic concept.

I do not agree with the philosophy that the aged receiving social security payments should be penalized if they earn outside money. It is foolish to retire long-developed skills. Too often our elderly are retired only into lives of boredom.

Some 8 million mothers *not* on AFDC do work. If the regulations permitted it, the mothers on AFDC might actually prefer work to full-time child care particularly if they can find suitable baby-sitters or could take advantage of day-care centers.

A few among the young have lost sight of the fact that there is dignity and honor in a job well done. For a very few, welfare subsistence has become a profession. They literally feel they cannot afford to take a job. The attitude of these few has triggered much resentment and criticism of public welfare programs in general.

The tragedy of the depression and attendant suffering led us to champion the *rights* of people —to a job, to subsistence, to medical care, to housing and clothing. But with these rights go responsibilities.

The able-bodied unemployed should be given opportunities to do constructive, useful work for the public welfare, if the private sector is unable for a time to absorb them. If society has an obligation to make certain that all of our citizenry enjoy the right to the essentials, the individual in turn has the responsibility to play a productive role in that society's affairs if he can.

The relief and welfare laws and their administration are due for an examination and overhaul in order that we may make certain that they are performing the functions for which they were established. They are supposed to be palliative in nature and not substitute for affirmative programs designed to bring workers back into useful employment.

I advocate this for two reasons. First, because the attack on these laws is virulent and sustained; too many people believe the wild accusations made about them. Secondly, because these laws are designed to help the helpless, we must keep their operation under constant surveillance to make sure that *all* the helpless are covered and covered adequately.

We also require more widespread information about the availability of help to those who actually need it.

Obviously, coverage in some instances should be broadened, and the Public Welfare Amendments of 1962 have contained pertinent changes in this regard.

To me the most significant change in the 1962 amendments was the one aimed to assist welfare workers cut red tape by establishing an advisory council to study and make recommendations to streamline the federal-state programs of public assistance and child care.

A major objective of the war on poverty should be to make inroads on the numbers of people on welfare by helping them help themselves.

One of the keys to accomplishing this is more skilled, trained effective welfare workers and case-workers. We now have *only one trained welfare worker for every 23,000 welfare recipients.* The Public Welfare Amendments of 1962 authorized grants to the states (but appropriations have been delayed) to encourage the training of more and better personnel to administer welfare programs.

We should attract better personnel into welfare work with higher salaries. We should also hire more of them, three times as many at least, even if it means some federal assistance. Too many dedicated social workers are immobilized by paper work and regulations.

A good social worker should not be chained to a desk. We should reduce the paper-work load to the point where professional counseling, guidance and therapy are possible.

To be effective, our social workers should become involved in basic education, home management, work attitudes, and specific work skills. The focus in welfare work has increasingly been to discover ways of raising the level of income and increasing the opportunities for employment. There is a greater need for the old-fashioned relief worker, or indeed, even perhaps the old political ward-heeler who found jobs for the poor and taught them how to hold them.

Politics have taught me the value of leverage in this general kind of work. We have always found that one good professional worker who is able to interest and organize a group of volunteers is worth twenty times his salary. When volunteers are well organized and are given intelligent direction they accomplish wonders. This happened during the recent nation-wide effort to administer the Sabin polio vaccine. This was organized by a few professionals; the work was done entirely by dedicated volunteers. I have very seldom seen a more smoothly run operation—and the cost was very low.

A few welfare workers—trained and highly professional—can help the poor help themselves through the application of the same principles of leverage on a neighborhood-wide basis. There is no reason why the elderly, or the disabled, or the temporarily unemployed cannot act as baby-sitters for fatherless families or as playground supervisors. Those with knowledge and skills can teach crafts and trades to others. They can help care for the infirm.

Most people who have no job want something to do. Even if unpaid, constructive enterprise always gives people dignity.

From 1945 to 1948 when I was mayor of Minneapolis I started a program of welfare rehabilitation. We had some good people on the staff. We went through the relief roll case-by-case and we started a program of training that enabled us to cut the roll down to about forty hard-core families —genuine unemployables.

At a panel at Howard University, Jacob R. Fishman, codirector of Howard University's Center for Youth Community Studies, advocated the extension of the same basic theory to disadvantaged youth. He said the following:

First, it will provide jobs for poor kids in a field that won't be wiped out by automation. Then it will help meet the needs in a field where more and more workers will be needed. And the disadvantaged themselves know the problems of the poor best and can best work with them and inspire a spirit of self-help.

I emphasize volunteer and semivolunteer work in the field of relief because it works. The Peace

Corps, which I called for back in 1959, has accomplished wonders overseas. A Domestic Peace Corps which I have since advocated may well accomplish as much here at home. It could draw from the experiences of those who have been overseas and from the skilled body of professional welfare workers.

There are any number of places where we may look for experience and new ideas in the war on poverty—particularly to help those on the relief rolls. For example, in recent years there has grown up in the United States a small corps of highly intelligent, dedicated juvenile and domestic relations courts. Every day, all day, the variety of dislocations and the dreary manifestations of poverty come under the microscopic examination of these courts on a case-by-case basis.

Orm Ketcham, a juvenile court judge in Washington, D.C., has been advocating an institution there which he calls "Domestic Engineers, Inc.," to provide training for unskilled and semiskilled workers between sixteen and twenty-one years of age.

This is the way he describes his idea:

Employment of unskilled or semiskilled youth between sixteen and twenty-one years of age is one of the great needs in any program to prevent delinquency in Washington.

I believe that there is a great unmet need for persons trained to operate household machinery and to perform chores new to modern suburban living.

It is proposed that these specialty needs be met by a semiprivate, non-profit corporation named Domestic Engineers, Inc. This corporation would provide training for unskilled or semiskilled workers between sixteen and twenty-one with preference being given to those referred by the Board of Education and the Department of Public Welfare, etc. . . . Calls from householders for service, if within the scope of services offered by the Corporation and at a location to which public transportation is available, would be accepted by the Corporation. Service would be provided by youths trained, directed, and paid by the Corporation. . . .

At or before age twenty-one the domestic engineers will be expected to either specialize and prepare for a self-employed specialty service status or develop a regular weekly clientele of his own willing to assure him steady employment as a general domestic engineer without the support and supervision of the Corporation.

As Judge Ketcham's suggestion demonstrates, there is a need to provide jobs for those on relief drawing unemployment compensation. Welfare in some great cities has become massive. In New York City alone 430,000 men, women, and children live on relief payments—more than the entire population of Louisville, Kentucky.

One objective of the war against poverty is aimed at rolling back these transfer payments. If our war is successfully waged, we may see the day when some of the relief programs, particularly unemployment compensation payments, may be substantially cut back.

Poverty is everyone's business. We are an interdependent society. Poverty is an infectious disease that can contaminate everyone. If for no other reason, those who have wealth and power today should remember how transitory riches and influence can be, and should lend their minds and hearts to the cause of eradicating poverty in America.

People in this country do have the right to the basic necessities of life. We must help those in need with an open hand and an open heart.

9 / *People for Jobs: The Urgent Crisis in Education*

A great many phrases are repeated so often that they have a tendency to lose their meaning. There is one, however, that becomes more meaningful every day as our society becomes more complex and the tasks that men perform to support themselves and their families require a more and more highly developed intellect. It is, "Ignorance is the handmaiden of poverty." The two go hand in hand.

The figures make this clear. Of families headed by a person with only a grade-school education, 37 per cent are poor. Of those headed by high-school graduates, only 8 per cent are poor.

In today's economy, a man must know more in order to be able to earn even a minimum living. He should certainly know how to read and write. Yet, as we are discovering, the American educational system seems to be turning out large numbers of functional illiterates. Today's rapidly

changing technology allows little place for these
people. Levels of skills that were sufficient for yesterday's labor market are either marginal today
or simply no longer marketable. Standards are
rising fast even in household and other so-called
unskilled work. There is less and less demand for
common labor.

At the same time failures of our educational
system breed failures in our social and economic
system—delinquency, unemployment, loss of productive and purchasing power, and an increase in
tax-supported assistance payments.

Consider the now highly publicized findings of
the President's Task Force on Manpower Conservation, released earlier this year. They tell a
shocking story of what poverty exacts of our nation's manpower resources. The Task Force found
that one-third of the nation's youth would, on
examination, be found unqualified on the basis of
standards set up for military service. Poverty is
the principal reason why these young men fail to
meet those physical and mental standards. Four
out of five of those rejected on mental grounds
were school drop-outs; one out of five came from
families that had been on public assistance in the
past five years.

Who are these young Americans who do not
even possess the minimal educational background
required to serve their country?

As the requirements of the draft vary, these rejects total anywhere from a quarter to a third of

a million young men a year. What a frightful indictment of the American educational system!

I am impressed by the fact that those are boys not really mentally retarded or physically handicapped. They are the products of poverty, of understaffed and ill-equipped schools, of broken families; the sons of fathers 70 per cent of whom never went beyond grade school.

The appalling Selective Service figures emphasize that poverty and lack of education are, in a non-biological sense, inherited. A key first step to be taken in combating poverty is to break this family cycle of ignorance by concentrating on the youth of America.

The disturbing thing about a conversation with a typical draft reject is his lack of initiative. These boys do not seem to care about their futures—whether they go to school or what kind of a job they might find. They are indifferent and unchallenged—at best unaware. At worst, they live in despair and pessimism.

This is the thrust of the President's message on poverty to the Congress on March 16, 1964, and the emphasis of the Economic Opportunity Act of 1964 which President Johnson recommended.

In his message, President Johnson said:

The young man or woman who grows up without a decent education, in a broken home, in a hostile and squalid environment, in ill health or in the face of racial injustice—that young man or woman is often trapped in a life of poverty.

He does not have the skills demanded by a complex society. He does not know how to acquire those skills. He faces a mounting sense of despair which drains initiative and ambition and energy.

The President went on to say:

First we will give high priority to helping young Americans who lack skills, who have not completed their education or who cannot complete it because they are too poor.

To break this recurring cycle of poverty, lack of education, and more poverty, it is not enough to work with school drop-outs and draft rejects. We must begin much earlier with the preschoolers. We should establish voluntary nursery schools in our slum areas. Children from these deprived neighborhoods are out of step from the first day of school; their home environment does not permit them to compete on an equal basis from the very beginning. Such nursery schools should involve the mother as well as the child so that she may assist in the educational process.

Not only must we begin education at an earlier age, but we must also provide an extended day, a longer week, and a fuller year. Only through such concentrated and sustained effort can we compensate adequately for the handicaps thrust upon these young people by their environment.

We must provide greater opportunities for after-school, evening, and weekend activities. Extended use of libraries, school shops, home-economics rooms, science laboratories, art and drama facilities, as well as the gymnasium should be made available to both youngsters and adults. Volunteers to help supervise the child's homework when neither help nor space is available in the home would be a worthwhile activity.

Instead of 180 days of school a year with three months of idle vacation time, we must extend the opportunities for individual remedial instruction and advanced study. This will help provide depth and variety to the total school experience. Saturdays and summers are also ideal times for children to go on field trips.

It is only by providing such attention to the child and exposure to the school that we can hope to really give these children an equal start in life. Such a concerted effort might modify behavior sufficiently to break the cycle of poverty.

To me it has never made sense to shut down and let our expensive school plants stand idle and unused for almost 4 months a year when we have a shortage of schools and teachers. Proper planning should entail maximum use of our school facilities and enable us to pay annual salaries that would attract and keep competent teachers working full time. Many of these teachers now take additional jobs in order to supplement their income. These positions would provide opportunities for many of our unemployed.

Voluntary participation of our young people in these added educational opportunities should

be encouraged. In the rural areas we have provided County Agricultural Extension Agents and
County Home Agents who have contributed greatly
to the education of the young. A School Extension
Agent could perform a similar function in our
urban areas.

Having close ties with the school, the educational program, and the home, the agent would be
able to contribute to the over-all development of
the child. Our youngsters would concern themselves more with extracurricular activities, community and neighborhood improvements, and
work opportunities which would provide useful
outlets for their energies.

It is significant that the Economic Opportunity
Act of 1964 begins with a Title I aimed directly at
our children. It provides for a three-phase work
training program for over 400,000 underprivileged
youth.

A job corps would enroll 100,000 volunteers,
ages sixteen through twenty-one, for up to two
years on conservation projects and additional
basic education.

A work-training program would assist in financing publicly owned (state and local) or non-profit
projects calculated to create employment and work
experience for 200,000 young people. These projects are aimed primarily at conservation, the development of natural resources, and creation of
recreational facilities. Federal financing of up to

90 per cent is provided for during the first two years.

A work-study program in the bill calls for payments for up to fifteen hours of work a week for 140,000 low-income college students.

I have worked since 1957 for the passage of a Youth Employment Bill to establish a Youth Conservation Corps and a program of local-area-youth employment. The primary effort in this kind of legislation is to develop sound work habits. As studies of the Civilian Conservation Corps of the 1930's have demonstrated, the primary need that existed among CCC enrollees was the opportunity to develop reliable, dependable, and mature work habits. The most fundamental of all so-called job skills is the ability to appreciate the value of work, hard work, for its own sake. An individual possessing a highly developed technical competence and lacking the ability to work hard is just as poor an employment risk as the most unskilled school drop-out. The personal qualities of reliability, maturity, dependability, and honesty far outrank any specialized technical ability that may be taught to a young worker.

This kind of legislation cannot, in any sense, be described as "make-work" or "leaf-raking." There is a great backlog of useful work to be done including about 8 billion dollars worth of programmed conservation projects. In tackling these, young people will acquire on-the-job skills.

The opposition to the Economic Opportunity Act of 1964 comes from the same people who opposed tax reduction and reform, legislation to foster educational improvement on the elementary, secondary, college and postgraduate levels, urban renewal, and expanded vocational-education opportunities. The same people opposed the Youth Employment Act and attempted to cut the entire manpower retraining program in half by reducing the authorization from four years to two.

In addition to complaining about the cost of the legislation, the opponents of youth training argue that this remedial measure takes place after the age of sixteen, when the damage has been done. This is quite true but rehabilitory legislation is not intended to be a cure-all. Attention must be paid to first things. We now have the opportunity to accept community responsibility for needs that require immediate attention and will show immediate results.

It is important to get young people off the streets and into productive work of some kind. The Economic Opportunity Act accomplishes this and creates better work habits and work experience. These programs will also train those involved for permanent employment as adults. This is no more expensive than an alternative welfare program and will do much to alleviate the problem of juvenile delinquency by instilling in our youth a sense of the dignity of work.

The high rate of drop-outs from our educational

system is frightening in its implications. Case histories like these from Public Affairs Pamphlet Number 346 tell stories that attest to the necessity for an all-out attack on the problems of education.

Mike is eighteen. He left high school a year and a half ago in the middle of his sophomore year. The immediate cause was an argument with a teacher over an unfinished assignment. Long before that incident, Mike had been staying away from school for two or three days at a time. Neither courses, nor extracurricular activities, nor his fellow students in the big school appealed to him. A bunch o' squares who don't give you no break'' was his opinion. Efforts on the part of his teachers to take an interest in him were met with sullen evasiveness. In the depressed, grey neighborhood where Mike, his sisters, and his mother lived (his father had long since walked out), it was a basic tenet that things could only get worse if anyone in an official position took notice of you.

Ruth also left school on her sixteenth birthday, but not because no one had made her aware of the importance of graduating! Her parents' greatest ambition was that their daughter enjoy the educational advantages denied them in the depression. Each month they had painstakingly set aside money toward her college tuition. Ruth had been one of the bright ones in her grade school class, but in high school her teachers complained that she was working far below capacity. In spite of, or perhaps because of, parental pressure for good grades, Ruth was failing three out of four subjects.

These children, like 30 per cent of all children who enter high school throughout the country, have turned their backs on one of the greatest advantages the United States offers its citizens— twelve years of free schooling.

There are two basic reasons for drop-outs : the lack of money in the home and/or the failure of the educational system to teach the value of education itself and to stimulate the young with a desire for knowledge.

As we investigate further, the correlation between education and poverty becomes clear. Of all families earning less than $3,000 in 1962, 61 per cent have a breadwinner who had gone no further in his education than elementary school. By contrast, only 7 per cent of these poor families have breadwinners with some college education.

A family headed by a person who has completed only eight years of schooling or less has more than one chance in three of being poor.

The facts show that education holds the key to escape from the mire of poverty.

An education is the best insurance policy against poverty our youths can have. It prevents them from being one-skill workers subject to the ravages of the machine. Education gives people mobility and a variety of employable skills.

Study after study proves that for every additional level of schooling completed, a man or woman may anticipate higher average incomes in the future.

Dr. Herman P. Miller has developed figures to

show average income for men aged twenty-five and over in 1959.

Education	*Average Income*
Elementary school:	
Less than eight years	$2,551
Eight years	3,769
High school:	
One to three years	4,618
Four years	5,567
College:	
One to three years	6,966
Four years or more	9,206

It is clear that education pays even for people doing the same kind of work. For example, a bus driver who had graduated from elementary school averaged earnings in 1959 of $4,400. A high-school graduate also doing a bus driver's job earned $1,000 more.

The importance of an education is highlighted by the fact that for today's college graduates, employment opportunities are generally excellent and pay-scales are constantly rising. But most young people who do not go through college suffer because they are undereducated to meet the skill requirements of today's labor market.

Tabulations indicate that the unemployment rate among technically-trained workers is about 1 per cent; among workers with some skills, such as truck drivers and electricians, the rate is about

12 per cent; but among unskilled workers it runs over 19 per cent. Under these conditions what prospects are there for the 42 per cent of Americans who fail to complete high school?

We are rapidly compounding this sliding scale. During the 1960's, the demand for professional and technical labor is expected to grow by a staggering 40 per cent, while the demand for unskilled labor is not expected to grow at all. This is in the face of an ever-increasing glut on the labor market of young people without any technical training whatsoever. Economists speculate that within ten to fifteen years present failure to develop employable youth will be ten times the problem it is today.

One of the ways we can help solve the coming shortage of jobs is by encouraging more education. The longer children are kept in school and off the labor market, the less pressure against the shortage of employment opportunities. At the same time our children will be acquiring higher degrees of skill.

The children of poor families need improved job and education counseling and youth-oriented employment services. Children raised in the bleak and unpromising world of poverty are surrounded by adults whose hopes have been destroyed, or never kindled; these young people need to be motivated and given the opportunity to participate in meaningful work experience.

I also suspect vocational training has a tendency to lag behind the changing and constantly up-graded skill requirements of the labor market. The President's Panel on Education is studying this matter. It may well be that the vocational efforts of the federal government, the schools, and business may have to revise and up-date these programs.

Huge efforts will have to go into education and vocational training, which have never had their rightful place in America's educational system, not only on the lower levels but on the high-school level as well.

Students should be given a far better idea about the special paths open to them. They need to be given more information about specific career opportunities and where and how they can obtain financial support for post–high-school education so that they can prepare themselves for these careers.

Guidance expansion will give additional meaning and hope to a child whose economic background is such that he is constantly laboring against pressures to become a drop-out.

Perhaps the greatest educational need is intensive and specialized reading programs, both in and out of school.

Not only reading but the basic mathematical and writing skills must be improved. These under-educated young are not as lacking in understanding as they are in the means to express their knowledge. It is this deficiency of a good back-

ground in the three R's which is their greatest
single educational handicap and one which prevents them from participating in many of the existing higher-level training programs.

The partial solution to this particular problem
has been previously mentioned—providing remedial programs and supervised study. An attack
should also be made by the employment of new
educational techniques. In this area the self-in-
structional devices or teaching machines offer one
approach which should be more widely adopted
as a supplementary method. While more experi-
mentation and research is needed, we do have sufficient evidence to know that if properly employed
they can make a major contribution, particularly
when used in remedial work. Teaching machines
also permit instruction in more advanced technical work with less reliance upon advanced reading
skills. Military and industrial training personnel
have demonstrated the advantage of such programmed training employing audio-visual aids
in teaching machines. We are permitting automation to create a large army of unemployables while
refusing to use these same automated techniques
to train our labor force.

In the fairly isolated environments in which
most of the youth conservation camps will be located, and with too few professional personnel
available, programmed courses can be of particular value. This is also true with the teaching of
adults where the privacy of response is a major

advantage. The poorly educated dislike participating in any program where their lack of education is embarrassing.

We must at the same time undertake the retraining of older workers who are continuously
thrown out of jobs because of automation and
haven't the ability to find new work in a dynamic
society. It is an old-fashioned notion that skills
and knowledge possessed at the age of 20 remain
undepreciated for a working lifetime.

The rate of obsolescence of skill and knowledge
is rapid, and will speed up, as automation and
cybernation continue their advance. It will apply
to a wider range of tasks, and to a much larger
segment of the labor force. Retraining and upgrading are growing problems. A highly skilled weaver,
displaced by automation, is only an unskilled, unemployed statistic somewhere else.

In addition to easing these dislocations through
strengthening the federal training and retraining
programs we must improve educational standards.
If we develop general educational levels retraining would not be so difficult for the displaced to
acquire.

Much of the acquisition of new work skills comes
on the job, not in a training school. A large part
of retraining is conducted by firms, by unions, and
by governments. But to be successful teachers must
be dealing with a literate and readily adaptable
people.

In stressing education as a means for escaping

poverty in material terms, I do not mean to under-
value the need to continue to develop the American culture. Man is more than an occupational
individual. He is a total personality. We must
not concentrate so hard on poverty of the pocket-
book that we neglect intellectual impoverishment.
We seek to improve not only earning capacity,
but cultural appreciation as well, so that all our
people may enjoy self-attainment and full expression.

In New York City there is a 3.8-million-dollar
program called Higher Horizons that is both seeking to break the lack-of-education poverty cycle
and at the same time trying to maintain all-round
intellectual values. Higher Horizons may well be
a model for other communities—one of the new
ideas we need in the war against poverty.

In the New York slums, perhaps because of the
sheer weight of numbers, the problems of education are all too acute and all too well known.
Higher Horizons is trying to bring academic light
into the life of some 99,000 children who come from
what the city calls "deprived" areas. The objective is to try to find and stimulate students with
college potential and to give these children intellectual motivation.

The program is being run by Miss Carmella
Mercurio. It provides 290 special teachers and 157
guidance instructors to add extracurricular matter to regular teaching routines. Miss Mercurio

says that the purpose is to promote "academic and cultural enrichment" through individual attention.

More than seventy elementary and junior high schools from a variety of neighborhoods participate. There is no set pattern. In one school it may focus on the more promising children—in another, on those who need the most help.

Miss Mercurio says, "If a child has never met anyone with even a high school diploma, he doesn't identify with people successful in academic areas. He doesn't have the motivation to complete school, to pull himself up."

She cites the examples of Randy Lewis, age nine, and his brother Ralph, age ten. They are third- and fourth-grade pupils in Public School 194 in Harlem. The boys live around the corner from school in a two-room tenement walkup, which they share with six other people, including two adult aunts. Their father, who attended P.S. 194 himself, works in Brooklyn and is away much of the time. The boys' mother is dead.

David Edelstein, the principal of P.S. 194, is trying to help Randy and Ralph rise above their environment. For a period of time Edelstein's thanks came in the form of more truancy. But now, suspicion gone, the school is virtually the boys' weekday home. They stay for a program that keeps them off the streets until supper time. Both the Lewis boys get special attention in their

school work and occasionally they are taken on
field trips or to colleges to see boys from similar
environments who rose above poverty and neglect.
Teachers also counsel parents in an effort to involve them both in their children and in neighborhood problems.

It is too early to tell just how effective Higher
Horizons will be, but Miss Mercurio knows what
the difficulties ahead of her students are. ''This
generation,'' she says, ''must prepare for jobs that
didn't exist in their father's day.''

As if the difficulties, and its present failures,
were not enough, the American educational system is now experiencing an enrollment explosion
which is severely taxing existing physical and
human facilities.

Urban school facilities are, and will continue to
be, the most crowded. Sixty-nine million children,
more than one-third of our present population,
were born between 1946 and 1962. They are now
of elementary- and secondary-school age. This
wave will begin to hit the colleges in 1965. Enrollment in elementary and secondary schools was
28.2 million in 1950 and 46.7 million in 1963. By
1970 it will be 53.2 million.

One of the problems of the poor is that, both in
terms of school facilities and teaching personnel,
the more run-down neighborhoods almost inevitably have the more dilapidated physical plant as
well as the lowest caliber of instruction. But, re-

gardless of the neighborhood, there is an urgent
need for more and better teachers and schools.

A suggestion I like is that in schools where there
is a shortage of teachers we have the more advanced children assist the slower ones. Children
learn readily from other children and those helping will enrich their own experience.

In order to instruct the huge masses of children entering the schools, we need thousands of
new teachers at all levels: elementary, secondary,
college, graduate. We also must have substantial
improvement of quality, particularly at elementary and secondary levels. Here, too, help from
the Federal government has been negligible.

Today, from all sources, we are spending only
about 5 per cent of our Gross National Product on
education. There must be a very large increase in
the public investment at all levels—federal, state,
and local—if we are to meet our present educational and training needs—to say nothing of the
explosion of the future. Improving education,
training and retraining workers, and vocational
training—these things obviously take money as
does the building of extensive additional plant
facilities. Traditionally, we have operated a public
school system. The necessary funds have generally
come out of the public sector.

Because only the Federal government has the tax
base to meet the cost involved, I see no alternative
but that it quickly become more deeply involved
with massive aid to education at all levels, and on a

crash basis. In spite of great efforts made by state and local communities—71,000 classrooms built annually during the last five years—little headway has been made on the backlog, to say nothing of future requirements. Federal help has been negligible despite legislation such as the Higher Education Facilities Act. We must get over the whimsical idea that the federal government can build highways or power plants at the local level without destroying democratic institutions, but cannot help build a school or assist in financing the training of teachers for our children. To me the 'control-of-education'' argument makes as much sense as saying that because the Federal government built the highways, it will usurp the function of the states or local communities in patrolling those highways against reckless drivers. Or that the Federal government will dictate to you what make or color of car you must drive.

I know of no one associated with the federal government, directly or indirectly, who has the slightest desire to control the curricula of the various school systems or who believes that federal control is desirable public policy. The question of what is taught in the schools and how is better left to the communities themselves, the school boards, teachers, and professional educators who must deal with these matters on a day-to-day basis. I know of no school district receiving aid under the federally impacted Areas Aid Program has ever complained of federal control.

As research investments are the key to increased efficiency and productivity, so increased investments in education are the key to the door through which the poor can escape from poverty. Education enriches the entire community, the whole nation. It enables us to lift the economic and cultural floor of our nation—so that even the relatively poor may not be as poor as their forefathers.

10 / Jobs for People: The Employment Crisis

According to economists, "structural" unemployment takes place when automation and new technologies displace wage earners. "Frictional" unemployment occurs when a wage earner is between or changing jobs. Not long ago, while speaking in northeastern Minnesota, I referred to structural and frictional unemployment.

There is a great deal of poverty and unemployment in northern Minnesota, principally because of massive shifts in the iron and steel industries. On the day I spoke, a middle-aged man came up to me. He was a member of the steelworkers' union. He said quietly, with the slight accent of a first-generation American, "Senator, that was a good speech. I'm sure glad I'm structurally unemployed, and not just frictional."

As I listen to the debate on poverty that is now beginning, I note that it is very easy to slip into an academic discussion, which may be fascinating to those who know the specialized language of economic scholarship, but is too often filled with a jargon that baffles most Americans. It is important that the discussion be carried on in terms of human problems, of the realities of the poor, and within a practical framework of what can be done about those appalling realities.

For example, there is the position that since the poor will always be with us we should do nothing. The country is prosperous, such theorists argue, and the poverty-stricken are too ignorant and too lazy to help themselves; since all men will never be equal in wealth, and as long as welfare programs and charity keep people from starving in the streets, we are doing enough. Their argument is that the government is already too big, and since the rapidly expanding economy appears to be making some slow inroads into poverty, we should leave well enough alone. Most Americans, I believe, reject this idea and agree that action on the federal level is required when the free play of the marketplace is unable to accomplish the results our people require, and when state and local governments cannot do the whole job alone.

It is true that the steady economic growth of our country has tended to reduce the incidence and the depth of poverty, and that even the most abject poor of today live better than their nineteenth-century counterparts.

Between 1929 and 1960, the total number of Americans living in poverty was reduced at an average annual rate of about 2 per cent. From 1935 to 1947, the annual rate of reduction was almost 5 per cent, due to the social reforms of the thirties and the enormous shot in the arm of the war economy. During the years 1947 to 1953, while, in general, we had reasonably high economic growth and employment, we slipped back to a 2.7 per cent per year reduction in poverty. And from 1953 to 1960, with rising idle plants and unemployment, the average rate of reduction in the number of families living in poverty had fallen to barely over 1 per cent.

Despite a booming economy today with nearly 70 million people employed, the hard knot of the poor stands in sharp relief against the incredible wealth of the country as a whole. It is simply not enough to say that their lot has improved.

The most tragic problem of the poor is their lack of real opportunity.

When I was in the Soviet Union in 1958, I became the first American holding high office to address the Russians on television. In the course of my remarks I used the word "opportunity." The interpreter looked puzzled. After the broadcast I learned that he knew of no equivalent Russian word for "opportunity."

The economic keystone of democratic government is the fact of opportunity, not some spurious opportunity of the few, but the opportunity for the poor to rise out of their poverty. Beyond acting humanely—and no self-respecting society can permit any of its children, its handicapped, and its elderly to live in abject poverty—the task of government must be to see that the way is open for those who have the ability to move upward to a better life.

There is another dialogue taking place concerning poverty that I find interesting because I believe that both sides are partly correct. This has to do with the problem of jobs for people.

The Senate Employment Subcommittee chaired by Senator Joseph Clark of Pennsylvania recently issued an excellent report called "Toward Full Employment." It demonstrates the relationship between our Gross National Product and the objective of full employment. It proposes that the year 1968 be set as a target date for reducing the rate of unemployment to 3 per cent.

In order to achieve this goal, the subcommittee estimates that the real Gross National Product must rise to 734 billion dollars, measured in 1963 prices. This implies an annual growth rate of approximately 4.6 per cent.

This is not an impossible achievement if we set out to accomplish it with realistic imagination and vision. Actually we exceed this rate during upswings in the economy. Over all, however, our growth rate has been only about 3 per cent.

There is general agreement that growth is the key to full employment, but the same cannot be said for those who are seeking the means to sustain that growth. In fact most economists are in absolute disagreement on the "how" of full employment.

One argument is that the way to create jobs for the unemployed is to increase purchasing power among the poorer segments of our people. This would be done by amending the tax laws to redistribute income. These economists would cut the share of the tax burden carried in the lower income brackets. In addition, this school of thought (which we might call the "consumption" school) would institute a massive public-works program and substantially increase welfare, social security, and unemployment compensation payments. The idea would be to stimulate purchasing power among the impoverished and enable them to spend more to satisfy their wants and basic needs. The resulting increased demand would, in turn, stimulate an even greater production and would create more jobs.

The other school (which I call the "production" school) would concentrate more on production itself by encouraging investment in new facilities, particularly in depressed areas. They argue that a solution in Appalachia and similar distressed areas is to encourage new industries, and consequently new jobs, to come into the area. They would attract new business, including the establishment of facilities turning out new products into depressed areas by offering attractive financing terms and tax concessions.

Opponents of the "production" school argue

that because we already have idle plant capacity in the country and enormous funds constantly seeking attractive investment opportunities, the net effect is to rob Peter to pay Paul. They say that establishing a "new" facility in Appalachia might take it away from, perhaps, Los Angeles, so that the net gain to the country is negligible.

I believe that policies borrowing from both theories can be intelligently meshed, because they are interrelated. You cannot increase the purchasing power of an unemployed miner in Appalachia (unless you use an out-and-out dole) without giving him a job. At the same time a production facility in Appalachia without both local and outside purchasing power to buy its production is senseless.

I cannot subscribe to the rob-Peter-to-pay-Paul argument, because it is founded on the fallacious theory that the American labor force is infinitely mobile. An area like Appalachia, where employment is desperately needed, would not be helped by putting a new plant in Los Angeles. It is a simple fact that the distances between centers of rapid employment growth are great. New plants have a tendency to locate in areas where there is a shortage of labor.

Most of the disagreement stems from both sides' tendency to think of the economy of the country as a single economic entity. It is true that for the country as a whole there is idle plant capacity. And substantial funds are indeed avail-

able for attractive investment opportunities. The
trouble is that the problems that exist in one part
of the country are not the same as those in another. Bankers might well be eager to finance a
manufacturing facility in Detroit or an electronics
plant in Los Angeles where a trained labor force
already exists and where community facilities
such as transportation, power, water, schooling
and cultural centers are good. But what about
Appalachia? Would the bankers care to finance
not only the new facility but, in addition, the necessary back-up community facilities like highways, hydro-electric power, and schools and training programs to remake unemployed miners into
skilled electronic technicians? Obviously not.

In the depressed areas, an obsolescence of available skills has frequently already occurred, and
the labor force may consist of skilled miners,
farmers, or textile workers without any market
for their abilities. In the booming areas a different pool of skills exists—skills that the new technologies, such as electronics, demand. Further-
more, in a boom area, the infrastructure is apt to
be more modern and plentiful—roads, railroads,
power, service facilities, as well as the schools and
other cultural and recreational facilities which
are always an attraction for new industry.

In short, the depressed areas are not in themselves competitive in attracting new industry, and
in turn new job opportunities. Enlightened public
policy must help them compete. Excessive unem-

ployment in this country has no one single cause nor can it be eliminated by any single cure. To reduced high unemployment in the distressed areas of western Pennsylvania, northern Michigan, Wisconsin, and Minnesota, for example, calls for specially designed measures to reform the economic base of each of these areas.

I do not quarrel with those who would concentrate on increasing consumption. It is simply not a complete answer. To break the back of chronic unemployment we must consider the individualized difficulties facing each separate locality, in addition to thinking of the economy as a consuming entity.

We all recognize unemployment as a colossal waste. It wastes productive capacity, as well as destroying purchasing power, and potential consumption.

Secretary of Labor Wirtz has pointed out that over the past several months America has lost more man-hours of production because of unemployment than because of all the strikes of the last thirty-six years.

Walter Reuther estimates that in the last ten years we have lost 25 million man-*years* of potential economic production because of mass unemployment. He says, quite properly, that an hour of human labor cannot be stored in a warehouse like a ton of steel, or even frozen like food. An hour of human labor must be used when available or it is lost forever.

We have poured down the economic drain 600 billion dollars in our potential gross national product which we could have created if we had had full employment and full production and an adequate rate of economic growth during the past ten years. This money represents our margin of progress toward better education, slum clearance, adequate medical facilities, highways, and all the other resources that we should be developing to improve the quality of our society. Full employment will bring us these resources.

No matter what political party we may belong to or what economic school of thought, we surely must agree that continued rates of high unemployment in America are an unacceptable drag on the nation.

But if it is easy to recognize unemployment as a drag, *present* rates of unemployment are only part of the problem. Unless we move swiftly, unemployment rates will be an ever-compounding evil.

Not long ago Secretary Wirtz testified before a joint Senate-House committee that to maintain unemployment at 1957 levels we should have created over 11 million new jobs between 1957 and 1962, because of new entrants into the work force. We fell short by 10 per cent. As a result, over 1 million new unemployed were added to the rolls in those years. The Secretary went on to say that between 1962 and 1967 the problem is going to get even tougher, because of the baby boom of the war and immediate post-war period. We will now need over 16 million jobs created by 1967, just to stay even with our present level of unemployment. If we fail at the same rate that we have been failing, we could slip to a level of unemployment in the United States of 8 or 9 per cent by 1967.

It is clear that there will be no solution to poverty with this kind of unemployment level. We must take immediate steps to secure these new jobs. We cannot wait until 1967 to see what kind of prophet Secretary Wirtz is.

Between 1960 and 1970, estimates are that 22 million jobs will be eliminated by automation and more efficient production techniques. At the same time an additional twelve-and-a-half million new persons will have moved out of classrooms and into the labor force for the first time. We shall have to provide close to 300,000 jobs per month just to keep up with the current effects of automation and new labor force alone.

Three hundred thousand jobs a month, just to stay even, is equivalent to a whole new industry the size of the entire meat-processing industry or all of the General Motors production complex per month. Put another way this means we shall have to find new jobs every single month for a group of workers the size of the population of Miami or Akron or Omaha.

The problem caused by the laying off of blue-collar workers by automatic machines and white-collar workers by computers is extremely difficult. Automation and cybernetics actually differ only as to the color of the collar worn by the worker

being displaced: assembly-line automation dis-
places a blue collar; cybernetics is the substitu-
tion of computers and other electronic devices for
white-collar workers.

Automation has been called a "monster" and
"without effective planning a real curse in this
society." Others say that automation and cybernation are really boons, that they mean more and
better goods and products at cheaper prices.

Clearly, to the displaced worker—blue or white
collar—automation is indeed a curse. Dislocations
are taking place and will continue at a high rate.
Automation and new techniques may outmode an
entire skill. Overnight virtually the entire work-
force of a town or even a region may be thrown
out of work. This is a new kind of unemployment.
These suddenly displaced workers cannot readily
move, as the very process of picking up one's
family is a heavy economic burden especially with
no guarantee of a job situation awaiting him at
the other end of the line.

But it is also clear that greater efficiency cannot be stopped. The massed intelligence of the
twentieth century has too much momentum. America is not going to be turned back to a simpler,
more understandable society.

Our gigantic task is to learn to comprehend
the consequences of technological change, and to
attempt to guide this fantastic power into socially
constructive channels. In his State of the Union
Address, President Johnson requested the ap-

pointment of a Commission on Automation and Technological Change for this purpose. Senator Hart of Michigan and I have introduced S.2298, a bill to implement the President's request by creating a Commission on Automation Technology and Employment to analyze every aspect of technological change. We must have much more solid information, in order to see to it that automation and cybernetics are encouraged to create new jobs, not more jobless. They must create boom towns, not ghost towns; build new factories, not simply retire inefficient plants. This commission must also inquire into the needs of tomorrow's economy, so that we will not continue to teach our people skills that are obsolete on the day that they finish their training.

We know that not all automation reduces employment. For example, we enjoy the world's largest communications system. It is a unique industry, both because of its rapid automation and because of the reaction of its employees.

Not long ago, even for local telephone calls, you would pick up the receiver and hear an operator ask, "Number, please." But, since 1920, the Bell Telephone System has been building the world's largest computer. We now dial local calls and many long-distance calls.

Today a telephone call can be made across country for about one dollar; in 1920 it cost $16.50. In 1959, the Bell System paid in 1.7 million dollars in taxes, whereas in 1920 they paid 27.5

million dollars. Today the Bell System has two-and-a-half times the number of employees it had in 1920. The System maintains more than 200 schools, constantly training some 5,000 new employees for future jobs. Although due partially to normal turnover, 50,000 new operators are hired a year as the nation demands expanding telephone service.

The telephone has automated rapidly. As a result, we have more and better service. Cheaper service has led to such expansion that the telephone is no longer a luxury. And in this case, at least, the consequence has been that there has been an accompanying increase in employment. This very expansion of use, not automation per se, has been the factor which has created the new employment.

But suppose the market for new telephones becomes glutted? Suppose rapid expansion is no longer possible? If the industry for some reason should stop expanding, automation and cybernetics would no longer result in new jobs. New telephone techniques would instead decrease the number of employees.

Last November Joseph A. Beirne, President of the AFL-CIO Communications Workers of America, told a congressional committee that he recognized that automation can bring long-term benefits and will raise standards of living. But, he said, planning should be undertaken to minimize the damaging effects on labor. This is the enlightened approach of the chief of some 380,000 workers who must contend with automation and cybernation.

We cannot afford to pay for long-range benefits by permitting short- or long-range misery.

The experience of the Bell System is encouraging because it shows that where new technologies help a business expand rapidly new jobs result.

But this is not a uniform situation. It is only wishful thinking to sit back and hope for the best.

The automobile industry is another huge part of our economy. In 1957 it required 310 man-hours to turn out an automobile. By 1963, when the industry was offering a more complex car, automation made it possible to produce a car in only 159 man-hours.

The plain truth is that at a time when our population is exploding and we need more and more jobs, the technologies of the space age enable us to turn out vast quantities of new product in fewer man-hours.

Full employment alone will not cure poverty, as long as workers receive inadequate wages and there are people who simply cannot work. But, at the same time, poverty can certainly not be cured without full employment.

The almost overwhelming task of finding jobs may well force us into solutions that tend to spread the available work around. One of these is the thirty-five-hour (or less) work week. Even a cut in the work week by itself would hardly be an answer to unemployment. As machines and computers do more and more of the work, it is essential that per capita purchasing power be maintained at ever-increasing levels to consume this increasing productivity. Present tax cuts and, hopefully, more to come, particularly in the low income brackets, will be of some help. In addition, through the minimum-wage laws and the collective-bargaining process, it will be vital to keep pay scales and take-home pay high. The idea that a "sound" economy depends on keeping wages down is an antiquated theory. A "sound" economy occurs when there are large numbers of workers producing and buying goods. They are the mass market that keeps industry going.

Automation does have some clear benefits. It has usually brought prices down sharply on some goods, even in an era of generally rising prices. From 1958 to 1963, for example, the following price changes in per cent took place during a general cost of living increase:

Automobiles	+ 2
Refrigerators	− 9
Television	− 7
Washing Machines	−10
Vacuum Cleaners	−15

In an expanding competitive market, automation appears in some respects as a blessing from the consumer's point of view.

During the same period the prices of services

such as hospitalization rose 32 per cent. Housing costs, where labor is a big ingredient, have doubled in recent years. Although it is no doubt true that the quality of service, particularly in hospitalization, has improved due to recent developments in medical science, these figures are indicative of an upward trend in the cost of personal service.

I have cited the decrease in the sales price for washing machines. But there is a human price being paid. I have visited a washing-machine factory where in one section of the plant there had been 125 or more employees. Due to automation the number of workers went down to five and then to three. Most of the 122 employees displaced in this particular factory have since found other, and more profitable, work; but some were hurt. Some paid the price for increased efficiency in washing-machine production.

The washing machine produced was an improved machine and sold at a lower price. It became a better consumer item; more were sold. The over-all impact was not to lower the gross national product, but to increase it. Gross National Product seems to be the best single index of the increasing or decreasing material well-being of the American people. Similarly, as more machines were sold, there was a corresponding increase in service and maintenance employment—a matter which puts a good deal of money into circulation, as any housewife knows.

Worker displacement is taking place throughout industry. For example, a new steel-rolling mill just installed by Jones and Laughlin in Cleveland, Ohio, operated by only a handful of men, can roll in one twenty-four hour period as much strip, as it took 12,000 men to roll in 1927.

New technologies and automation are not confined simply to improve techniques in existing industry. They can open up entirely new fields, creating thousands of new jobs. Television and the whole synthetic fabrics field are but two examples.

Thus technological advance and rising productivity on the one hand have many human payoffs in higher incomes and consumption, longer life, reduced suffering and illness, reduced drudgery and greater leisure. On the other hand, society cannot ignore those who are run down by the juggernaut of efficiency.

There is some evidence that the pace of automation is increasing ever more rapidly, and that the dislocations ahead of us will be more severe. But the Council of Economic Advisers argues that the evidence so far indicates there has not been a net over-all reduction of total employment caused by automation and cybernation.

I am not certain that the hypotheses on which the Council's argument is based are valid. But here is the core of their argument:

Historically, there is surely no evidence of any inability of demand to rise along with productive capacity, or of any permanent inadequacy of total job opportunities. Rather, our technologically progressive economy has brought higher output and incomes, and more and better consumption and investment, along with the voluntary decision to take some of the fruits of progress in the form of leisure. Since 1929, for instance, output per worker has almost doubled. If total demand had not grown since 1929, and if we were still producing the 1929 level of output, using present methods of production and the present shorter work week, it would take just 26 million workers to do it. This would leave two-thirds of our present labor force unemployed. Instead, the demand for output is almost three times as high, and employment is 50 per cent higher than in 1929. If total demand had grown since 1929 only as fast as population, 46 per cent of our labor force would now be unemployed as a result of the higher productivity.

Clearly, the increase in total demand for our potential output is the factor that has reconciled advancing technology with rising employment.

Automation and the shifting character of new industries and technologies have an impact not only on individuals but also on entire areas.

In the last ten years, total non-agricultural employment has declined in Rhode Island, Pennsylvania, Michigan and West Virginia. But it rose 40 per cent in California, 65 per cent in Florida, 80 per cent in Arizona, and 97 per cent in Nevada. These changes take place as changes in types of jobs occur. Farmers and farm workers have declined 40 per cent in only ten years, and there has been a similar decline in numbers of locomotive engineers, railroad firemen, textile weavers and spinners, telegraph operators, and fishermen. At the same time there have been significant increases among teachers, engineers, and draftsmen.

Certain skills become obsolete; at the same time demand for completely new skills arise. Trouble occurs, however, because it is not a simple matter to transform a fisherman into an engineer.

The general upgrading in skilled employment has been rapid. Unskilled farm and non-farm workers who accounted for 30 per cent of the labor force in 1900 made up only 8 per cent in 1960.

The major impact of automation falls on those least able to bear the burden—the less-skilled, less-educated and, as a consequence, the poorest among the labor force. We are eliminating the bottom rungs of the ladder. We have not as yet devised satisfactory methods for relocating displaced workers, or for starting new workers, on the higher rungs.

Displaced workers do not find new employment immediately. Time is required for matching skills with new employment. There is no quick and easy way to shift from one job to a new one, as a report from the Council of Economic Advisers indicates:

The average duration of unemployment was 11.6 weeks during the period 1955–57, when the over-all unemployment rate averaged 4.3 per cent. And, during the boom years of 1951–53, when the unemployment rate averaged 3.1 per cent and the number of unfilled jobs very probably exceeded the number of unemployed workers, the average duration of unemployment was still 8.7 weeks.

So far we have been discussing structural unemployment at the expense of other types of unemployment.

Seasonal unemployment probably accounts for as much as 20 per cent of total unemployment. Although it requires attention it is a less critical problem than structural unemployment. There seems little that can be done to eliminate it except to assist those employees who wish supplemental work to find jobs.

Cyclical unemployment is the economists' term for jobs lost by general recessions. It no longer monopolizes our attention because our concern with the structural problem has grown, and because we have experienced modest success since World War II in limiting the severity and duration of recessions. Monetary and fiscal policies and public-works programs, to some degree, have kept general business declines within bounds. Meanwhile defense spending has been pouring a stabilizing 50 billion dollars or more annually into the economy.

As already mentioned, there is also frictional unemployment as employees move from job to job. It commands an impressive percentage, possibly one-third of our total unemployed. It is of relatively shorter duration as workers change jobs, advance up the occupational ladder, move from place to place, enter or leave the labor force. A substantial proportion of frictional unemployment is voluntary. To the extent that frictional unemployment is not voluntary it can be helped in the same ways as dislocations of structural unemployment.

There are a great many things that can be done to alleviate the problems of unemployment, regardless of kind. Obviously an economic climate conducive to full employment will enable displaced workers to find new jobs more quickly. The recently passed tax cut is helping to create such a climate. Its purpose has been to increase demand levels and investment incentives and bring the over-all level of unemployment down to at least 4 per cent. Tax reduction should create new jobs and expand employment in most industries. Cuts have accrued to 50 million individuals and 600,000 corporations. Their direct rise in after-tax income is being translated into purchasing power for all kinds of goods and services, in turn creating new jobs and reducing unemployment substantially.

The tax cut will not be a complete solution by any means. First of all, even a 4 per cent rate of unemployment is unacceptable. I suspect that even 3 per cent, the goal of the Senate Employment Subcommittee, represents more than the number of unemployables and those between jobs in this country.

The report of Senator Clark's subcommittee states that "Countries such as Sweden, France, West Germany, and Japan, have, by aggressive monetary, taxation and expenditures policies maintained a high level of production and unemployment levels below 2 per cent by U.S. definitions.'' It may be that a flat comparison is not a fair one since our problems may be different from theirs. But the figures show that an unemployment level of under 2 per cent is not an unrealistic objective in contemporary Western civilization.

There is a need for strengthening the present machinery to help the unemployed find jobs quickly.

The record of the Federal-State Employment Service improves yearly. Since 1961, it has increased its non-farm job placement by 25 per cent.

The vocational retraining program of the Department of Labor will assist some 148,000 workers in training or retraining during fiscal year 1964 in skills as diverse as drafting, stenography, nursing, auto repairing, and metal working. The program will be expanded to provide training and retraining for 288,000 workers in fiscal 1965. The recent broadening of the Manpower, Development and Training Act will sharpen its effectiveness in coping with unemployment among low-skilled workers and youths. An important part of this program will be the provision of adult-education courses in fiscal 1965 for 60,000 persons who are unable to acquire industrial skills because of a lack of basic literacy. Vocational training will be provided for 85,000 unemployed youths.

Passage of the Youth Employment Act would give us conservation work camps and work projects for 60,000 young people in 1964 and for over 100,000 in 1965.

Training Americans is a good investment. In Minnesota during the early 1940's I was associated with the War Production Training and Re-employment Program of the Works Projects Administration. We set up vocational schools all over the state. I had 30,000 people in my schools. These were people that everybody said were just no good.

One night a few years later a man came up to talk with me at my church. He began the conversation with this question, "Do you remember me?"

I said, "Well, I remember you; but I do not recall your name." He gave me his name and said, "You got me off the relief rolls up in Stearns County and put me into a vocational training school. The Government paid me $60 or $70 a month. I know there were an awful lot of people who were saying this was a waste of money. But I would like to tell you something. I am now the supervisor out at Honeywell."

Honeywell is one of our large industrial electronic plants, and a top defense production plant.

He told me that he had a boy who had just finished 40 missions in the Air Force and two others who were in the Navy.

His final remark was, "I just want to ask you one question: Do you think the government wasted its money on me?"

But these training programs are relatively small. Contrast them with the current number of unemployed—over 5 million persons—and the million-plus new persons coming into the job market every year.

Automation should be used on a larger scale to intensify the collection and the rapid exchange of improved information on current job openings, by skill, number, and locality. Automating this exchange of information would be an instance where the use of new technology could be a boon to the work force.

Programs to assist the geographical movement of workers, such as relocation loans, should be expanded. When jobs are found there must be efforts to match that job with a worker who is presently unemployed.

Employers should be encouraged to give advance notice of plans for mechanization or automation that will eventually displace substantial numbers, as well as providing alternatives available to the displaced worker and apprising them of the steps management is taking to minimize the problems that will occur.

In general, the problem of finding and filling jobs demands a large-scale effort in apprenticeship training, vocational education, and retraining.

Another suggestion that appeals to me is the use of the tax structure to encourage the creation of jobs themselves. We have, in the past, utilized tax relief through accelerated amortization of plants and equipment to stimulate the creation of new production facilities, and might well explore the possibilities of extending this measure.

Where a depressed area is involved, and where a new facility can demonstrate that it will in fact create new employment opportunities, we might permit such a business to list its new factory as an expense rather than capitalize a certain portion of its initial investment. This means that a businessman could deduct these amounts for tax purposes. In addition we might consider reducing, for a period of time, the tax on those profits which might be attributable to the new employment created. Both types of tax incentive would be feasible from the accounting point of view and neither would unduly complicate the filing of returns. This might help depressed areas compete for new facilities and job openings.

Automation, cybernation, and technological improvements all help produce real wealth more quickly and cheaply. That is a fact of which we must not lose sight. If they are not an unmixed blessing, then we must simply concentrate new efforts to ensure that the families of the displaced are given every opportunity to fit themselves into a new role in the economy. We cannot tolerate a

situation in which better living standards for the
many are largely paid for by the loss of jobs and
income of the few.

The requirement for massive planning has been
recognized by industry itself. John I. Snyder,
president of U.S. Industries, has said:

The total solutions to our unemployment problem, I
believe, are going to depend on total planning directed
towards two major ends: first, the creation of new industries in this country; and, second, the creation of new
markets for our products.

We must do more to make available to the
civilian-based economy the results of the enormous amount of defense-related research and development. The Defense Department alone spends
some 9 billion dollars a year for research and
development and the federal government as a
whole about 16 billion dollars including the Federal Aeronautics Administration and the National
Aeronautics and Space Agency. This is about 75
per cent of all research funds expended in the
country. Although Admiral Rickover has estimated that the bulk of human knowledge doubles
every nine years, it is too often concentrated in
sectors which are not immediately conducive to
creating jobs. As the amount of knowledge accu-
mulates, we must spread it into the private sector
in order to develop an ever increasing number of
new products and hence expanded employment.

The computer now guides capsules into outer

space and monitors changes inside man himself; it runs assembly lines and mixes as many as 500 chemicals in an automatic fertilizer plant; it translates Bibles and checks the age of brandy; it handles reservations for airlines and processes payrolls, inventory, and purchase orders for giant corporations; it even creates new computers. If we are to take advantage of this technological revolution and utilize its nature and power, we must start now. To shape this revolution to our own ends will require the most intelligent co-operation among management, labor, and government. The final test of our society may well be whether or not we can create the political and economic devices necessary to master and guide the forces of science.

11 / *The Federal Partner*

The solution of the poverty problem is not possible without the full participation of all elements of our society. Government alone cannot do the job, nor can it be accomplished entirely by the private sector of the economy. To achieve the goals set forth in this book co-operation and partnership must replace the too-prevalent feeling of hostility and suspicion between government and private industry. It is the purpose of this chapter to discuss the role of the Federal partner in the attack on poverty and perhaps shed some light on apparent federal dominance in certain areas.

Defense procurement and space research and development could be powerful Federal tools for the attack on poverty. Government spending presently amounts to approximately one-sixth of the Gross National Product. The defense and space budgets alone, principally through purchases in the private sector of the economy, now approach one-tenth of the entire Gross National Product.

Clearly, where and how this money is spent has a direct bearing on the pattern of abundance and the pattern of poverty in the United States.

There are very distinct patterns indeed. In 1963, the Department of Labor listed 517 areas of the United States as examples of substantial and persistent unemployment. Twenty million people live in these sectors, with an unemployment rate of over 9 per cent—far in excess of the average rate for the nation.

In 1960, Candidate John F. Kennedy said:

> Economists tell us that an unemployment rate of six per cent is the danger signal. When a community passes that point it is officially regarded as an area of "substantial labor surplus." If it remains there it is entitled to special Government help through defense procurement and other programs.

And President Kennedy, in 1961, encouraged the Department of Defense to follow a policy directive (Directive for Military Procurement No. 4), under which they were to attempt to place contracts in areas of heavy unemployment.

In August 1962, I presided at a hearing by the Senate Select Committee on Small Business on government procurement programs as they related to distressed areas. One of the witnesses was Harold W. Williams of the Area Redevelopment Administration. According to Williams, only 3.7 per cent of defense spending was in redevelopment areas, although they contain 19 per cent of the nation's population and still produce about 10 per cent of the nation's goods.

The American taxpayer is the man who pays the defense bill; but he also pays the bill for unemployment relief in the chronically distressed areas and it is costly to provide unemployment compensation, direct relief, food stamps, public works, area redevelopment grants, and loans. And there are also the severe local and state tax losses, from unemployment itself, which throw a heavier burden on those state and local taxpayers who are employed.

Ron M. Linton, then Director of Economic Utilization Policy of the Department of Defense, testified at the hearing as to the specific impact of one Department decision on the problem of employment and unemployment:

Senator Humphrey: I thoroughly agree with you that the defense dollar is not the full answer to the unemployment problem. But I want to tell you, neither is unemployment compensation, and it is a whole lot better to get a defense dollar in there with a job than it is to get a weekly check on unemployment compensation. . . .

Also, it is the view of some of us, as this testimony reveals, that with a defense contract in an area, it tends to bring with it other community development and other business development. I believe this is a fact . . .

Mr. Linton: We estimate that for every defense production job in an area, it will create three other jobs in the area in service jobs.

Senator Humphrey: . . . if I were Secretary of Defense . . . my straight-line thinking would say, Look, what we want to do is be able to get these items for the military establishment as cheaply as we can and as high quality as we can . . . That would be good if the only department in this government were the Department of Defense. . . .

But what about the cost to the Department of Labor and the Social Security Administration, the Department of Agriculture, and all the other departments of government who are feeding the unemployed, giving them medical care, providing grants and gifts, giving them unemployment compensation? Why don't we add that all up in this contract business?

The reason we do not is because everybody is guarding his purse rather than somebody taking a look at the total picture. . . .

Mr. Linton: I would say that because I am a non-career government worker, I essentially agree with you. That is the reason I went into the Defense Department. About three days after I got there in June 1961, one of the first cases I ran into was where a contract was awarded to a low bidder, who was low bidder by $250,000. The result of the award was the second low bidder closed his plant and 1,200 people were put out of work. I did an exercise for the particular Secretary who made the decision showing that the $250,000 the Department saved actually cost the government $950,000 because of those lost jobs. The reply of the legal department was, "That is fine. We agree with you; we have looked at these things but we can't figure these things into our costs because the Congress said we can't."

Thus, the apparent "saving" by the Department of Defense of $250,000 on this decision actually cost the American people $700,000. Such thinking clearly places departmental bookkeeping over national objectives.

Thanks to the dedicated work of a handful of men in the Economic Utilization group located in the office of the Assistant Secretary of Defense, an increasing amount of defense procurement is being placed in industries located in distressed areas—at no extra cost to the Department of Defense.

According to the latest estimates, these defense "set-asides" for depressed areas may be expected to rise from the present 100 million dollars per annum to 200 million dollars in the near future. This means that those bidding for prime government contracts are being encouraged to produce in distressed areas. But compared to our total defense budet of 50 billion dollars, even 200 million dollars is a miniscule figure—less than 1/2 of 1 per cent. Despite the strenuous efforts made to encourage the large prime contractors to place more of their sub-contracts in distressed areas, a relatively small percentage of the total procurement dollar goes to create new jobs in high-unemployment areas.

The appropriations committees of Congress have specifically directed that no defense procurement decision be made that would result in any extra cost to the Defense Department.

Defense Secretary McNamara on many occasions has said: "Defense Department policy, as in the past, is to buy what we need when we need it, at the lowest cost to the government quality and delivery schedules considered."

46 per cent of such work, and 28 per cent goes to the New England and the Middle Atlantic States.

In the new technologies, it is absolutely vital that those competing for production business have close and frequent access to the minds who are conducting the advanced research work in their fields. Inevitably, this means that jobs follow R & D investments. For example, in the immediate area around Massachusetts Institute of Technology and its Lincoln Laboratories—large recipients of research contracts—over 400 new companies have sprung up over the last few years. A recent decision to center the electronics research effort of NASA in the environs of M.I.T. is eloquent testimony to the drawing power of a great complex of researchers. In a very real sense, the rich get richer and the poor get poorer without a coherent and determined policy of providing a more balanced and systematic allocation of R & D funds.

While those who have been wise and energetic enough to make a major effort to secure Federal R & D grants should not be penalized for that initiative, it is clear that in the future a conscious effort should be made to develop other complexes of research and its follow-on production in other areas of the nation. Such an effort will require not only Federal encouragement, but also a great deal of state and local initiative.

More can be done to encourage the flow of the intellectual products of federally sponsored research and development into the private sector. The Commerce Department is commencing a major effort in this area—an effort which can help to stimulate the growth of civilian-based industry and of jobs not dependent directly on the Federal dollar.

Federally sponsored research data should be reviewed with the object of declassifying as much of it as possible, and making it freely available to civilian business and industry. Thus, the benefits of Federal research—paid for by all our citizens, wherever they may live—can be spread around the country and throughout the population, in terms of better and cheaper goods and more job opportunities.

Automation and cybernation may be helpful in achieving permanent prosperity, and are not mere threats to jobs. We know far too little about the possibilities for using the computer for job expansion.

We have already examined the possible use of automation and machines to speed between the various state and Federal employment offices the exchange of information about the availability of job opportunities and personnel to fill them.

We should also consider letting research contracts now to determine the ways in which computers can be used on a large scale to maximize our knowledge of the economy in order to detect danger signals in time to take preventive action on the part of both industry and government. Computers, too, give promise of assisting in the decision-making for the allocation of Federal investments or encouraging Federal investments in old and new programs.

And as a stimulator of the private sector of the economy, the Federal use of the computer could be a dramatic herald of unmet needs, untapped markets, unrealized sales, unfulfilled recreational spending.

Computer models can stimulate the dynamics of free enterprise in a way which will offer maximum reliability in predicting the economic future.

Heretofore, economic statistics gathering has been segmented and tardy. A few elementary steps have been taken, under the auspices of the U.S. Bureau of the Budget, to avoid needless duplication in circulating Federal questionnaires and the like. The emphasis has been to avoid imposing needless requests on the private economy. This is a sound, but too limited, objective.

There will always be some guesswork, some risk, some unknowns, inherent in free enterprise, but the computer can help us minimize avoidable mistakes and assist decision makers in both government and private enterprise to determine upon actions that will stand up to the tests and strain of time.

Because an ever growing domestic economy and full employment are fundamental to a successful war on poverty, we must constantly seek to stimulate and increase our markets overseas. Here again, an affirmative and constructive partnership between government and management can do much to encourage job-producing exports. Time and again, our businessmen are beaten out of sales because of a lack of sufficiently aggressive government backing, through credit guarantees and other means.

The Federal partner needs to be much more aggressive and imaginative in encouraging foreign investment sales by American business. We must be able to match credit guarantees against credit guarantee, tax incentive against tax incentive, if we are to stay in the fierce competition for markets in the underprivileged areas.

We do not, except in rare cases, issue long term guarantees insuring repayment of credits advanced to private institutions such as banks making investments overseas. Usually we limit long term guarantees to those against expropriation, war-risk, and the convertibility of funds. England, France, Germany and Japan, among other countries, issue unconditional guarantees of repayment, frequently as much as 90 per cent of the investment made.

For example, suppose a South American government wishes to purchase a large amount of railroad equipment in order to rehabilitate its railway system.

To accomplish this, the South American government might apply to private banks in London for a credit. If a large percentage of the credit was to be spent in England for equipment, the British government would guarantee a long-term private loan.

On the other hand, should the South American government wish to purchase American equipment, it could not ordinarily expect to secure a long-term credit except through our A.I.D. program. Should A.I.D. approve the project, the American taxpayer would foot the bill since the cash would be loaned directly by our government.

As a result, the taxpayer in countries such as England, is relieved of the cash burden of such investments which are made instead by the private sector. At the same time, exports are stimulated which, because of long term credits and favorable terms given, very frequently put businessmen from these guarantor countries at a highly favorable competitive advantage as against American businessmen.

I believe that this aspect of our international program is long over-due for review and change.

While we are asking American wheat farmers to cut down on production, Canadian wheat farmers —selling wheat to the Soviet Union—are being encouraged to plant more wheat. While we were debating whether or not to authorize sales to the Soviet Bloc, others had stepped in and pre-empted much of the market.

Farm prices and farm income, as well as jobs in American industry, are directly affected by the government's activities to stimulate or to hamper exports.

The question of protective tariffs is pertinent to increasing overseas markets. Obviously we must buy if we are to sell. And we must think very hard, when considering the erection of tariff barriers or quotas, about the possibility of losing export markets.

Some degree of protection is often required in order to make possible a genuine and equitable negotiation with a nation whose products may be severely harming one of our domestic industries. Certainly we cannot permit the dumping of excess goods on the American market at prices below the normal market level.

But, by and large, the problem of excessive imports can be handled by quiet negotiations and by using the competitive strength of our industry. While wages are high, by comparison with the world level, the training and reliability of American labor is as good as, or better than, any in the world. Our interest rates are relatively low and should stay low. Indeed, the American economic system provides the cheapest rate on money of any economic system in the world. The compound interest rate, which most of our foreign competitors have to pay, frequently offsets any wage-rate advantage that may exist.

Also, we do not have to import as many raw materials as the other industrialized countries. And we have a huge domestic mass market where we can experiment and try new products. All of these factors, in short, give us great competitive advantages in protecting American jobs against excessive imports, and permit us, therefore, to sell to others without hurdling excessive barriers to our own exports.

I believe that the coverage of the Federal Minimum Wage Law should be extended to include millions of low-wage workers who are not now protected by the $1.25 minimum. The areas covered by the minimum wage should be broadened. For example, the 1961 amendments to the Fair Labor Standards Act, which raised the Federal minimum wage to $1.15 an hour, also increased the percentage of retail clerks covered by the Act from 3 per cent to 33 per cent. Even after the law was passed, one-fourth of retail workers still earned less than $1 an hour.

An expanded public works program is clearly indicated, particularly those efforts which will tend to increase the vitality and the productive capacity of the private sector, or which will contribute to education, conservation, and recreation. More roads, water, and sewage-disposal facilities are still needed in many distressed areas. The population growth is simply outrunning the hospitals, schools, libraries, and recreational facilities of every major city. And the outdoor recreational resources of our state and Federal parks and forests have not been able to keep up with the expanding needs of our people.

There is no question but that a war against poverty in the United States must involve the expenditure of Federal funds—particularly in those areas where the instrument of the Federal government is best adapted to accomplish necessary work.

12 / *The Abundant Society:*
A Partnership in Knowledge

While the programs suggested in preceding chapters are aimed at solving the current problems of the poor, it is imperative that our proper concern for those who are suffering not prevent us from looking into the future as best we can and trying to devise the best possible long-range plans. If, as Santayana once wrote, ". . . those who do not know the past are doomed to repeat it . . . ," it is equally true that those who ignore the future are its certain victims. While the past is fixed, the future depends on what we are and what we do to prepare for it. The continuous and concerted attention to immediate needs must not be used to excuse a lack of vision.

It is true, of course, that the contemporary world is confronted with a multitude of problems. These problems cannot be avoided or ignored, and the attack upon them, one at a time as they become clear, is one of the marks of a civilization that is

187

still fighting for its ideals. Our pragmatic approach to past difficulties has resolved many of
those problems, but we cannot expect to achieve
utopia with every gain. History doesn't stand
still when a danger is averted or a problem is resolved; new problems always arise. We are
morally obligated to continue this war on poverty, not only to improve the condition of the poor
but to insure the well-being of future American
generations as well.

Contemporary poverty's two faces are equally
ugly. There are the traditional reasons for poverty: prejudice, ignorance, ill health, the thousand
and one accidents which can change a life of comfort to iron-bound hardship. Remedies for these
conditions are as many as there are causes and
only a fearful lack of courage, determination, and
wisdom in our society can prevent us from discovering and applying them. The present emphasis
on deepening our concern, in which this book will
hopefully be a factor, should indicate that apathy
is rapidly being overcome.

The other face of poverty is less familiar—and
more dangerous. Because of automation and our
increasingly complex civilization, a large part of
the poor are trapped below, and increasingly apart
from, the majority of our population. While those
above a certain point in the income scale are included in that mass of society which allows for
upward movement, those below the poverty level
not only do not participate in the movement but

are being forced into a position where they cannot. We may find ourselves in a society with hardened class lines—a society which America has never experienced. Even now it may account for the mutual bewilderment, at best, and unswervable hatred, at worst, when representatives of these two classes try to communicate. They often fail because they are viewing the world from points poles apart. This emerging trend can be a disastrous one. In Dante's *Inferno,* the motto on the gate of Hell was "Abandon all hope, you who enter herein." The inhabitants of America's underworld of poverty must never be subjected to such a paralysis of helplessness and hopelessness.

There is abroad in the land today a widespread unease; for while we may be proud of our progress, and while we are the wealthiest country in the world there is still a pervasive feeling that something has been lost. Something has gone wrong. Nor is this feeling simply nostalgia for a past viewed through the wrong end of the telescope, seen as a life of charm and comfort where in actuality it may well have been a life of hard work and discomfort. For whether or not our view of the past is accurate, the fact remains that our vision of the past is a set of values which, in large part, is lacking from contemporary life. We live in an age which has become increasingly complex; in an age which has seen America move from the periphery to the center of world affairs. At the turn of the century, we were basically a rural people; now we have become a country of city- and suburb-dwellers. All available evidence shows a continuous acceleration of change. The city of yesterday is the metropolis of today, and the metropolis of today will constitute the megalopolis of tomorrow.

We are entering a revolutionary period as profound in its implications as the Industrial Revolution itself. This is the revolution of knowledge. Just as the religious, political, and social establishments that had guided men's lives for centuries were wrenched and sometimes torn down by the brute force of economic power, so the institutions of twentieth century life face the test of this new revolution. The catalyst for this revolution is scientific research, three quarters of it supported and paid for by the American government.

The speed with which knowledge and the technical know-how to accomplish change are growing is astonishing—much more rapidly than we are able to adapt our political and economic institutions to accommodate the new knowledge.

Admiral Hyman Rickover's estimate that the sum total of human knowledge doubles every nine years was supported by the testimony of John H. Rubel, then Assistant Secretary of Defense, on May 20, 1963. Rubel pointed out that knowledge is increasing so rapidly that the experience and training received by today's engineers in their schooling becomes obsolete in a matter of ten years. Rubel feels that the new knowledge can literally solve any problem society can devise, if there is what he calls the "social need." Social need is his term for an objective which the people demand to be accomplished.

We have now reached the point where our new knowledge may be utilized, if properly harnessed, to solve sociological problems "to repair," in Rubel's words, "to elevate, to amplify the quality and excellence of the environment in which we work and live." But the art of politics lags behind technological know-how. The ability to solve technical problems is, perhaps, less important than the understanding of what our technical problems are and the political decisions as to what directions we want our society to take.

We have been discussing one of the great opportunities of man's history: the elimination of poverty from American society. While such a victory is more remote for most of the rest of the world, it is possible here because of the enormous productive capacity which the current explosion in knowledge has brought about.

We do have the resources, more than enough resources. At the height of the pre-Depression boom in 1929, our Gross National Product was 104 billion dollars. Today it is *six times as much*. It is over *ten times* what it was thirty years ago, and still climbing fast. The Federal Reserve Board places our gross national savings and investment money at over a staggering *three-quarters of a trillion dollars*. This is half again as much as it was only five years ago.

Consider also that we are spending today some 50 to 60 billion dollars on the defense budget, depending on what one includes in "defense" spending. The administration has begun a careful cutback. Obsolete government plants are being closed, and production facilities are being shut down as our arsenals become full. The President has drastically rolled back the production of fissionable materials. Roswell Gilpatric, the former Deputy Secretary of Defense, looks forward to a possible 25 per cent cut in projected defense spending over the next five years—if the Soviet Union continues on the path of slowing down and cutting back its own arms programs.

Suppose, in addition, the Soviet Union were to join us in a major effort for safeguarded and inspected disarmament. If it were to come suddenly, the American economy would be hard put to cope quickly with a sharp cutback in arms procurement unless we were to plan now to re-direct our energies. This is a matter of urgent priority. Our country cannot be put in the position of possibly rejecting the path to peace through safeguarded disarmament simply because we could not afford the economic adjustments that a slow-down or shut-down in defense expenditures would require. Planning now for the conversion from defense industry to peacetime industry is an absolute essential.

A concentrated and successful attack on the inequities in our society can be financed well within the resources of the cutback discussed by Mr. Gilpatric—much less the utilization of our other enormous resources.

Yes, we have the resources—more than ample resources. And the Federal government should not pay for everything; it cannot itself do all the planning. What it can do is provide the leadership to call for a joint venture to war on poverty. It can provide the leverage to stimulate the private sector to make the necessary investments in time, energy, and, finally, in dollars.

If then, through our combined efforts, we deal effectively with poverty as we know it now, what will the future be like? Although the future has traditionally been the province of utopian thinkers and science-fiction writers. In retrospect, it is surprising how often what seemed to strain our credulity has become accepted as commonplace. What we can do now is make the desired goals as specific as possible and encourage the discovery and actualizing of the means for their attainment. This is a difficult task; it is hard to visualize something which does not exist, and the boldness to imagine a society very different from our own is a rare quality. The history of the last fifty years seems to assure us that whether or not we imagine a change, we will nevertheless experience it. Only if we wait passively for the future to come will we be its victims rather than its masters. Our technological advances, our deeper insights, our knowledge, and the results of contemplative thinking might themselves be a clue to what the future might be like, if once we take the reins in our hands and direct it as befits a free people. For no matter how complex the world might be, it is still *our* world, and its complexity is in great part *our* creation. The forces which direct our destiny remain blind and frightening only if we refuse to open our eyes and exert our own strength in control. The deepest concern of America is not only for its poor but for all its people; not only for the economic problems of the moment, but for life in all its dimensions and the possibilities of a richer life in the future. For the problems of the future as seen and known *now,* are our problems. The war on poverty will not be truly won until we determine that poverty must be replaced not by barely tolerable conditions, but by an abundant life.

We can plan our communities so that the natural beauties of the landscape and waterscape are not only left undestroyed, but enhanced. The architecture of the large cities must be improved so that there is enjoyment to contemplating the cityscape. We need wide avenues, a multitude of open spaces such as plazas, parks, squares, buildings which complement each other, neighborhoods which in their diverse ways cater to a full life for all their inhabitants, young and old, whatever their income level.

We must rethink our transportation needs to better suit the means to the ends. A combination of public and private transportation is a must for a country with a population which is expected, conservatively, to double by the end of this century. Within these two categories we must require a great variety of techniques. Transportation for long distances has different requirements than for short distances; getting to work need not be done the same way as going shopping. To design one kind of vehicle to accomplish all these results most efficiently as we now attempt with private cars, seems ridiculous. We must create a public transportation system which will serve many of these purposes and which will enable us to get from place to place in comfort, and with speed and safety. Again, the benefits of such accomplishment would be shared by all.

We must create not only larger educational facilities but those which will give our citizens the skills and training which will enable them to develop all their capacities. We must learn to use our leisure so that the reduction of the work schedule is looked on as a boon rather than a threat. The variety of recreational and cultural pursuits must be as large and as accessible as possible. Technological innovations should be sought to make this variety possible. If there is good rea-

son for dissatisfaction in being treated as an inter-
changeable part in a mass audience now, how much
worse it will become when the population doubles. We should seek to create a diversity of large
and small audiences, to increase the multiplicity of
participating groups, and should develop the means
which makes this not only possible but economically desirable.

Mass production, using modern scientific techniques, can be made very flexible in its output.
Since the products are to conform to the demands
of the consumer, production facilities should be
created to respond with a wide range of outputs.
The variety of products now available to us is
amazing, but if we wish to, we can make not only
new ones but products which are almost unique
responses to single requests. This desirable variety applies to both goods and services. Nor would
such a goal for our national product be wasteful.
Quite the contrary: since the products would meet
precisely the purpose for which they were needed,
wastefulness would be eliminated. Only in a relatively crude technology is standardization of the
end-product a necessity. From the factories' point
of view it is more efficient to produce only left
shoes of one size and style but is obviously sheer
waste. In an advanced technology, responsiveness
is increasingly built into the system. Lest this
sound too mechanical, let it be understood that I
mean responsiveness to individual purposes and

needs, not only in goods but in recreation, culture, and knowledge, as well.

Reproductions of art works, reproductions of books, books on microfilm, as well as on paper, books that are electronically coded on magnetic tape; techniques for transmitting this information from place to place; methods of pursuing special subjects, of getting information quickly and easily and amassing it properly—all these should be easily available, from the need for a specialized recipe for the housewife to a need for the most abstract kind of statistics; all can be developed so that they are available to every home, as television and telephones are now.

Shopping might easily be handled through communication media rather than personal visitation. A complex communications network could explain what is available where and how and why, just as easily as laborious and lengthy trips.

These verbal pictures of what might come to be are not simply fanciful. If we want such a society, we can have it. In the creation of such a future, the employment problem as we currently myopically view it will no longer exist. This peaceful equivalent to our previous war efforts can have much more beneficial results. Under the pressures of such needs we can find ways of training on the job, because positions will demand to be filled.

Although some of the possibilities of remaking our country may sound fantastic and utopian,

they are not. The immense resources of science
place them well within the range of feasibility.
The important question which remains to be determined is are we strong enough, brave enough,
and persevering enough to alter our lives and em-
bark on the roads which will solve our problems?
Will we have the combination of imagination and
courage to live up to the traditions of our own
heritage that has raised us to our present state.
Our predecessors, as far back as the founding
fathers, possessed these virtues. Are we of their
stature? Our answer must be that we can make
life in the future still richer, more diverse, more
enjoyable than it is now. Unless we think about
how it can be accomplished and set out to accomplish it, we shall never know the answers to
these questions, and in ignorance we shall be the
poorer; and this poverty will extend not simply to
those who are labeled poor for economic reasons,
but to all of us.

Index

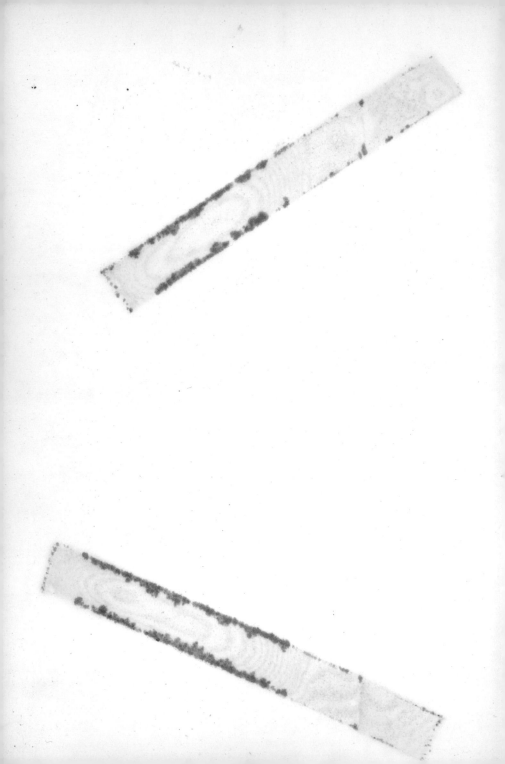